IDEAS FOR PE GAMES

KS1

P1 to 3

Author
Elizabeth Pike

Editor
David Sandford

Assistant editor
Dulcie Booth

Series designer
Anna Oliwa

Designer
Anna Oliwa

Illustrations
Ann Kronheimer

Cover artwork
Andy Parker

Designed using Adobe Pagemaker
Published by Scholastic Ltd, Villiers House, Clarendon Avenue, Leamington Spa, Warwickshire CV32 5PR

1 2 3 4 5 6 7 8 9 0   1 2 3 4 5 6 7 8 9 0

British Library Cataloguing-in-Publication Data
A catalogue record for this book is available from the British Library.

ISBN 0-439-01825-0

Contents

Introduction

WHY TEACH PE GAMES?

Young children are naturally physically active, and by teaching games in a structured manner we channel energy and enthusiasm in a positive and rewarding way. Skills taught well at an early stage will enable children to take part in a variety of games later on in school life with confidence and increased skill. Reception children will vary physically in height and weight, and will range in physical ability from those who are already showing signs of co-ordinated movement to those who have very little control over their movements. By introducing them to more formal activities we give them an increased opportunity to practise, to gain control and to learn.

The importance of helping young children to become physically fit cannot be underestimated – even very young children should become 'puffed' at some stage of each lesson. Apart from the obvious medical advantages, children gain a huge satisfaction in recognising their own progress and in feeling good about themselves.

Games lessons are a specific part of the curriculum, but they also provide opportunities for young children to reinforce other learning areas. For example, hearing the names of various parts of the body mentioned regularly can link with science work, and plotting children's progress in a table or as a graph can be used in maths lessons.

WHERE TO TEACH GAMES

Games teaching can take place in a variety of areas within the school environment. Most of the activities in this book can be taught in a school hall, on the school playground or other hard-surfaced area, or on the school playing field as appropriate to your particular situation. Some activities such as those involving bouncing may be difficult to teach on a playing field that has a soft surface, although if necessary this can be overcome to a certain extent by making sure the balls you use are well pumped-up. If an activity in this book is specific to an area of the school this will be specified in the 'Resources and class organization' section of the activity itself.

Clothing and kit

Many schools operate a uniform system which covers PE lessons. However, it is of great importance that teachers recognize their own responsibility with regard to safety and clothing. Shorts and a T-shirt are a sensible start, but when games lessons take place out of doors in colder weather it is important that young children begin the lesson wearing a warm jumper and trousers over this clothing. Very young children are limited in the extent to which they can keep warm through physical activities, and the need to maintain the 'enjoyment factor' is vital if children are to look forward to games lessons.

Footwear in a games lesson should have some flexibility, and plimsolls are a sound option. Many youngsters may prefer trainers, but if these are to be allowed they should be of the kind which permits movement on the ball of the foot. Generally, trainers with soles that can be bent when the shoe is held in the hand are best for games lessons; 'fashion' trainers with rigid soles are not suitable and should be avoided.

Jewellery should be taken off for the games lesson but problems do arise when children have recently had ears pierced or cannot take off a ring because it is too tight. Problems such as these can be overcome by putting lightweight surgical tape over ear-rings or sharp rings during games lessons.

Basic equipment

It is important to build up as large a variety of equipment as possible for children to use. It is not necessary to have large numbers of each type of equipment, but the basics will need to cover:

- Balls – these should be of at least three sizes: small, medium and large, and ideally should vary in material. Sizes for the younger age groups should range from the size of a football down to the size of a tennis ball. Popular materials include sponge, plastic and rubber and can either be solid or filled with air.
- Beanbags – these are a good alternative to balls for some activities.
- Bats – should include round, short-handled wooden and plastic varieties and short tennis rackets. Special infant rackets are available, which have shorter handles and a larger hitting area.
- Sticks – this may include wooden or plastic shinty sticks and hockey sticks.
- Obstacles – a variety of sizes of hoop are essential, as are skittles.
- Circular markers or cones – these will allow you to set out specific courses or playing areas for mini-games or aiming practice.

Size of equipment

Young children will need a variety of sizes of equipment to take account of individual differences and to prepare them thoroughly for a number of different activities. Many schools will be in a position where they do not have a similar-sized piece of equipment for every child in the class. This can be overcome by setting tasks where the size of the ball or bat does not matter, by working with groups doing different activities or by working in pairs. The activities in this book take this into account and will give guidance on how to organize this.

Organization of equipment

When placing equipment on a playground or field before a lesson, it is important to consider the space available, the quantity of equipment and movement of equipment. The use of large hoops to keep balls from rolling about is useful, and has the advantage of holding balls of similar or different sizes, depending on the tasks you intend to set for that lesson. When children collect equipment it is a good idea to send them in groups to one area, or to send them to a variety of areas to collect what they need. If the class are standing in pairs, in groups or in lines it is sometimes helpful if you roll balls along the ground to be gathered by the children.

Familiarization of equipment

It should never be assumed that young children can use bats and balls correctly or that they have control of their bodies. The warm-up activities (see Section 1) give ideas for very specific tasks which will enable children to improve their ball control and motor skills through running, stopping and balancing, as well as warming up their bodies for the main activity of the lesson.

Organizing the lesson

A games lesson should begin from the moment you tell the children to get changed. If they are regularly given a short but adequate time to change (for example, tell them you will count slowly to the number 25), are given clear instructions about where to stand or sit when they are ready, and if the movement from classroom to games area is conducted in a well-disciplined manner, then the children will be ready to work within an atmosphere that will enable them to learn more efficiently.

It is not always necessary to gather the children in front of you when you wish to change or extend an activity. If they are to use the same equipment and the instructions are short then you can teach from a spot where all can see you. However, when it is necessary to gather the children around you, it can save time and keep children warm if you have a regular routine which they use in doing this. For example, ask them to join a partner and stand one behind another in a line – the pairs having been arranged before the lesson.

Any activity taking place in pairs should involve all the pairs facing in similar directions in order to avoid balls being thrown across the pathway of different groups. With a large class and a small area it may be useful to number children and have half the class doing the activity whilst the other half are watching, after being given a specific brief to observe a certain part of the activity.

Activities concentrating on ball skills can be done individually, with all the class starting at one side of the room and progressing to the other side on your command. You should tell the children about height and distance of throws, bounces or kicks. This has the advantage of reinforcing the idea of control at all times.

Lesson structure

A games lesson should be divided into four parts. The warm-up (see Section 1) should never be missed out as it is part of the safety aspect of teaching games. Ideally, the warm-up should be followed by skill-based activities which will usually involve children working individually or in pairs. The third part of the lesson should consist of activities which encourage co-operation and teamwork and will give children a chance to put into practice some of the skills they have learned. Finally, a short cool-down activity should be given which will enable the children to slow down and prepare them to work in a more sedentary manner when they are back in the classroom.

Teacher demonstration

Teacher demonstration of an activity can serve several purposes. Children often learn more quickly if they can see an example of good practice; they sometimes need a pause after hard physical exercise and a short demonstration will usefully fill this gap; and it is sometimes quicker to show a group of children what you wish them to do than to try to explain it to them.

Left- and right-handedness

In most classes there will be a mix of children who are right-handed, left-handed, or even able to comfortably use both hands for a task. It is important that you regularly demonstrate throwing and batting activities with both right and left hand. Whilst it is not necessary to be able to demonstrate a complete throw or hit with your non-preferred hand, as long as you can hold the equipment and show the correct stance with arms, feet and body, this will be enough to enable children to learn. It is also a good idea to ask children occasionally to use their non-preferred hand for some tasks – this helps with control and is a very useful skill when they reach the age of playing full team games.

Beginning the lesson

It is not usually enough to begin the lesson with one quick warm-up activity. The purpose of these activities is to warm the muscles, to prepare the joints for movement and to practise hand-eye co-ordination through using equipment in a structured way. Therefore, a number of different activities should be used in the warm-up session (see Section 1).

Teaching skills

A theme should be planned for a lesson or series of lessons and skill-based activities should be chosen accordingly (see Skills grid on page 64). However, it is often necessary to combine practice of more than one skill, and this can easily be done by concentrating on one major skill and introducing teaching points covering other skills to individual children as required.

If you are choosing a theme for a lesson, make sure that you use a warm-up activity that works the whole body before you choose any themed activities to ensure that the children are properly warmed-up before the main part of the lesson.

Ending the lesson

After a games lesson, which may involve many different physical activities, it is important that children go through a short time when their minds and bodies can slow down as they prepare to engage in more sedentary tasks. Cool-down activities are an excellent way of gathering the class and giving their minds and bodies a chance to slow down. You and the children should realize, however, that these activities need to be done very slowly in order to achieve the desired effect.

To give variety at the end of the lesson, some gymnastic-type movements can be used to achieve the same effect. Stretching movements of all kinds are good, as are slow walking or running movements – leaving the field or playground in a controlled manner assists the cooling-down process.

Adverse weather conditions

Even very young children should be encouraged to enjoy outdoor games in the winter months, although sessions may have to be shortened with groups of children who are unable to sustain longer periods of activity in the cold.

Even so, it is not necessary to change the content of a games lesson completely if it needs to take place indoors. Careful planning and organization, and some alteration to the tasks given will ensure children get regular games teaching through the winter.

How the activities are organized

The activities in this book are organized so that you can plan a lesson or series of lessons with the minimum of searching. Warm-up activities have been grouped together in Section 1, as planning is likely to begin here for individual lessons. Sections 2, 3 and 4 cover Invasion games, Striking and fielding games and Net and wall games

respectively. Each of these sections is subdivided in order to separate tasks which involve one or two players and group activities which involve more than two players. On page 64 is an easy-reference Skills grid, which can be used as an aid to planning a term's work or a series of lessons with a particular theme.

Photocopiable pages

The photocopiable pages at the back of this book can be used in two ways. They can be used to support other curriculum subjects such as science, reinforcing the ideas behind the activities, or they can be used specifically for games work, either as an introduction or ending to a lesson in the classroom, or to plot progress during activities taking place outside. For example, 'My warm-up chart' (page 54) could be used as an aid to practical work and could also be used for assessment and plotting the children's progress.

Assessment could take place at the end of a period of several weeks when the children have regularly practised the activities. As there are a number of different kinds of activity, you could concentrate on a different type of discipline for each period of assessment chosen. The 'My progress chart' chart (photocopiable page 55) can be used to log children's progress over the course of the year.

Very young children need regular practice to thoroughly learn the names of parts of the body that you will mention during games lessons, and at an early stage activities such as a game of 'Simon Says' as part of a warm-up, followed by completing the 'My body' sheet (photocopiable page 56) will help to reinforce earlier learning. Photocopiable page 57 ('Name the equipment') is another sheet which can be used as an extension of a games lesson when the children have had a chance to familiarize themselves with the variety of equipment they will use.

These sheets can usefully be used immediately prior to or after the practical lesson to support and reinforce any learning.

Warm-up activities

The activities in this section may be used in any order. Use them at the beginning of a lesson as a warm-up, or at the end as cooling-down exercises. When warming up, it is not always necessary to begin with a task that involves a lot of running. Running tasks should be separated to some extent so that the children build up to running at faster speeds towards the end of the warm-up session.

Warm-ups can take place in the same area as you are teaching the rest of the games lesson. If using the school field, make sure any balls are well pumped-up; this will make any bouncing activities easier.

As the children learn more varied warm-up skills over a period of time, you may like to introduce the 'My warm-up chart' (photocopiable page 54) as an ongoing means of allowing children to plot their progress through the activities in this section.

The activities in this section focus on:

- using a variety of equipment
- moving in different directions
- moving at different speeds
- rolling, catching and throwing exercises
- co-operating with other children
- using the available space.

Roll and hold

Resources and class management

Children work as individuals if enough balls are available, or in pairs if balls are in short supply. Each child or pair will need a ball, these need not necessarily be of equal size; copies of photocopiable page 56 (for 'Now or later').

What to do

Ask the children to collect a ball, either individually or in pairs as appropriate, and then to find themselves a space to stand in. Tell them to hold their ball with both hands, and ask them if they can roll the ball up and down one leg and then do the same with the other leg. The ball must stay in contact with their body all the time, and they can only use their hands to do the rolling. When they have had sufficient time to practise this, ask them to try and roll the ball around their waist area, again emphasizing that the ball should stay in contact with the body at all times. This may be enough for very young children, but older children should be asked to see if they can roll the ball over their shoulders and across the back. Point out that they may have to let go of the ball with one hand in order to manage some of these tasks. Ask the children if they can think of other parts of the body they may be able to roll the ball over, such as the head or bottom. Finally, ask the children if they can roll the ball around their whole body without stopping or dropping the ball.

Objectives

To enable children to:

- practise control of a large ball
- increase body awareness
- experience contact with a ball using several body parts.

Cross-curricular links

Dance

Using simple movement patterns.

Gymnastics

Using space safely.

Differentiation

Younger children, or those who are physically less able, may use a slightly smaller ball or reduce the number of body parts they try to roll the ball around.

Now or later

- Instead of keeping the ball in contact with the body at all times, you could ask the children to hold the ball at arm's length and, using one hand then the other, to try to move the ball in a circle around their body. This can be further developed by asking the children to use one hand then the other to pass the ball between their legs and around to the back of their body. Emphasize that they should try not to drop the ball and should try to keep it moving all the time.
- Back in the classroom, the children can work on 'My body' (photocopiable page 56) to reinforce learning of the names of the parts of the body from the lesson.

Roll and run

Objectives

To enable children to:
- practise gathering up a ball
- experience changes of speed when running
- focus attention on the ball.

Cross-curricular links

Maths

Estimating and measuring in a practical context.

Gymnastics

Performing basic skills in travelling.

Dance

Changing the speed and direction of movement.

Resources and class management

Children work individually or in pairs. Each child will need: one large ball (or one ball between two children if equipment is not readily available).

What to do

Tell the children to hold the ball with either their right hand or left hand as feels most comfortable. Right-handers should have their right foot behind them as they stand and left-handers should have their left foot back, as shown below. Show the children how to bend both knees and, at the same time, swing the arm holding the ball back behind their body. Ask them to roll the ball along the ground and, when it is a short distance away from them, to run after the ball until they are slightly ahead of it. They should then use their feet to turn around and face the opposite direction, then bend and gather up the ball with both hands. After practising several times, ask the children to see if they can wait until the ball rolls further away from their body before they begin to run. Tell the children that the ball should be retrieved as quickly as possible each time, so that as it rolls further away they should run faster to catch the ball up. If the children are working in pairs, they should take turns to roll the ball and gather it up, swapping after each collection.

Differentiation

Young children may initially need to use both hands to hold the ball, but they should still be encouraged to hold it to one side of their body as they bend their knees.

Very able children should start by using the shorter rolling distance in order to warm up properly, but should be encouraged to move on to rolling longer distances to retrieve the ball quite quickly.

Now or later

As children become better at retrieving a large ball, reduce the size of the ball. This serves two purposes: firstly the smaller ball will roll faster if given the same push by the child, and secondly it requires more co-ordination to retrieve a smaller ball. Some children will be able to retrieve a smaller ball with one hand, which is good practice for later fielding and throwing activities.

Underarm duo

Resources and class management
Children work in pairs. Each pair will need one beanbag. You will need copies of photocopiable page 57 (for 'Now or later') for each child.

What to do
Split the children into pairs, and label the children in each pair 'A' and 'B'. Ask the children to spread out, with all 'A' children facing in one direction and all 'B' children facing their partner approximately three strides away. Tell the children that they are going to practise throwing and catching underarm.

Ask all the 'A' children to hold a beanbag in their right hand or left hand. Right-handers should place their right foot back and left-handers should place their left foot back. Show the children how to swing the arm holding the beanbag back behind their body and then swing it forward releasing the beanbag. Show how if they release the beanbag too soon it will be too low for their partner to catch, and if they release it too late it will be too high. The second child should be instructed to reach both hands forward at chest height, and as they receive the beanbag to bring it towards the centre of their body. If necessary, the catcher can move their feet or reach up higher than chest height with their hands to catch the beanbag, but encourage the thrower to be as accurate as possible to avoid too much movement by their partner. Encourage the children to practise throwing and catching the beanbag between pairs.

Finally, after they have had a chance to practise throwing and catching and are confident with both, tell the children that they should try to throw and catch the beanbag without stopping between each throw and without having to move too far in order to catch it.

Differentiation
Young children may at first need to shorten the distance between themselves and their partner.

More able or older children can increase the distance between themselves and their partner – they could be shown how to increase the speed of the underarm throw by increasing the speed of the arm action as they swing it back.

Now or later
- It is a good idea to use other equipment, such as quoits or different-sized balls with different textures. This gives children valuable practice in getting used to using lots of different types of equipment in the warm-up time, and allows them to observe how they may react differently when being thrown. Older children will be able to tell whether they have to adjust the throw, and how they do this to accommodate different types of equipment.
- Photocopiable page 57 ('Name the equipment') provides an opportunity for the children to reinforce their learning back in the classroom.

Objectives
To enable children to:
- experience different-shaped equipment
- practise aiming at a specific point
- improve their throwing stance.

Cross-curricular links
Dance
Changing rhythm, speed, level and direction of movements.

Throw and catch

Objectives
To enable children to:
- anticipate the fall of a beanbag
- judge the height of a throw
- practise throwing skills.

Cross-curricular links
Gymnastics
Linking skills and actions in short movement phrases.

Resources and class management
Children work independently. Each child will need a beanbag and a stopwatch with a second hand or other suitable timer. Beanbags can be substituted for sponge balls or quoits if there is not enough equipment to go around.

What to do
Ask the children to stand in a space of their own and to face you. Ask them to throw the beanbag into the air – they should throw it upwards as straight as possible, and for the first two or three attempts should not throw it too high. At this stage the children do not need to catch the beanbag. Practise the technique until the children can confidently throw the beanbag straight upwards.

When they are confident with throwing, show the children how to cup their hands with the fingers spread and how to reach up to catch the beanbag before it drops to the ground. As they improve, they should be encouraged to throw the beanbag higher and higher, still thinking about throwing it as straight upwards as possible.

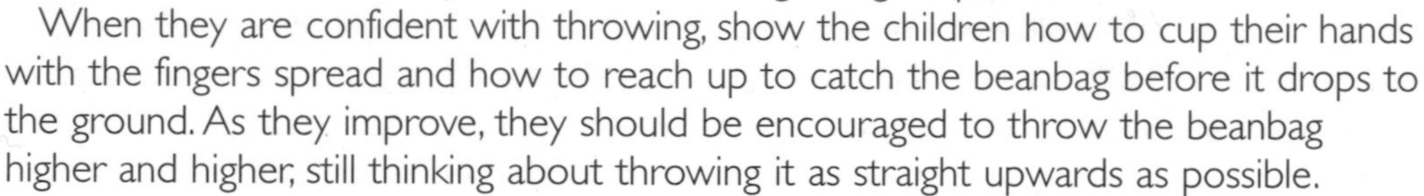

Finally, tell the children that you are going to time them for one minute, and they must count the number of times they can throw and catch the beanbag in that time. At this point, encourage the children to think about how they should throw in order to complete as many throws and catches as possible in the time allowed. The children should realize that in order to get as many throws as possible they should not throw the beanbag too high.

Differentiation
With a very able or older group of children it is a good idea to practise this activity in pairs. Tell pairs of children to stand side by side, with one beanbag between two. One child throws the beanbag up, and the other child has to catch it. Alternatively, exchange the beanbag for a small ball which is more difficult to catch.

Variations can be introduced by telling the children to let the ball bounce once before it is finally caught.

Now or later
Ask the children to work in pairs and collect one beanbag between them. Tell them to stand four or five strides apart. As one child throws the beanbag up in the air, the other runs in and catches it. It is important to emphasize that the child who is running should not begin until the beanbag is in the air, and that they should be careful to avoid colliding with their partner.

Bouncing bonanza

Resources and class management

Children work in pairs. Each pair will need one large ball between them, which should be pumped up hard enough to enable bouncing techniques to be practised. This activity should ideally take place on a hard surface.

What to do

Ask children to find a partner and to go and stand in a space approximately four strides apart, facing one another. One of the children should be holding a large ball. Tell the children holding the balls that they should make sure they have one hand on each side of the ball with fingers spread. One foot should be in front of the body to enable the weight to be more easily transferred from the back foot when the bouncing takes place. Tell the children to look at a point on the ground about halfway between themselves and their partner. They should then 'push' the ball hard towards the point on the ground, transferring their weight from the back foot to the front foot as they do so. Make sure that they know that when bouncing the ball they should not bounce it too hard, as it may hurt the other child. The child receiving the ball should be told to watch the ball carefully and reach both hands out to catch it once it has bounced, then to bounce it back to their partner using the same technique. In the early stages there will be a gap between each bounce, but as the children become more familiar with the activity they should be encouraged to keep the bouncing going without too much of a pause between receiving the ball and bouncing it back to their partner.

Differentiation

Young children or less able children will find this activity easier if they can see a mark on the ground where they are to aim when bouncing the ball. This can be done by using chalk to mark a cross at the halfway point.

More able children could place a small hoop between them and use a longer working distance, with the object now being to make the ball bounce inside the hoop before being caught.

Now or later

This activity is a good way to lead into working in a group of three. The third child should stand in the middle of the other two children with a gap between the others and facing the person with the ball. This child should try to intercept the ball as it is bounced between the other two children. Tell the child with the ball to aim at a spot immediately to the side of the child in the middle; if done successfully the ball will bounce too low for the child in the middle to catch it, but will bounce in the correct place for the child at the opposite side to catch.

Objectives

To enable children to:

- practise aiming techniques
- co-operate with a partner
- learn the skill of bouncing a ball.

Cross-curricular links

PSHE

Playing and working co-operatively.

Science

Knowing that pushes and pulls are examples of forces.

Hoop la!

Objectives

To enable children to:
- practise hoop-rolling techniques
- warm up arms and shoulders
- work co-operatively.

Cross-curricular links

Gymnastics

Finding and using space safely; developing and using a range of skills and actions.

Resources and class management

Children work in pairs. Each pair will need one hoop between them. These can vary in size, but should be large enough to go over the children's shoulders.

What to do

Tell the children to find a partner and to collect a hoop in their pair. They should then find a space and stand facing each other about five paces apart. The child holding the hoop should stand with their right or left side facing their partner. They should stand the hoop upright and place their preferred hand flat on top of the hoop. At this stage the other hand can be used to support the hoop. Show the children how to press down sharply with the flat of their hand on the hoop to propel it towards their partner. The receiving partner should reach out to catch the hoop as it heads towards them before it falls. When they collect the hoop, they should lift it over their head and body before stepping out of it, then they should turn sideways and roll the hoop back to their partner. Children may need to practise the rolling of the hoop so that it travels in a straight line. If the hoop does not roll straight at the beginning, encourage the children to run and try to catch it before it falls to the ground.

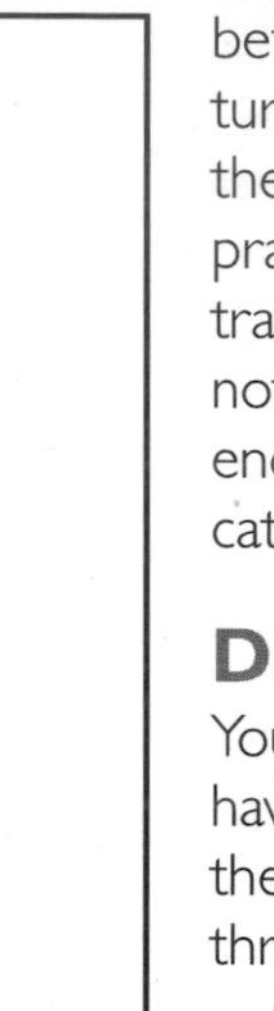

Differentiation

Younger children may find it easier to have a shorter distance between themselves and their partner – say two or three strides.

Older children can be given extra tasks to do with the hoop after it has been collected, for example stepping into the hoop and bringing it up over the head and body, or placing the hoop flat on the ground once received and jumping in and out of the centre of it twice.

Now or later

Children should be given one hoop each and, using the same technique, be asked to keep the hoop upright and rolling as they run alongside it. This can be developed so that, working in pairs again, they can run along with the hoop for a short distance before rolling the hoop on its own to their partner. This series of movements enables children to warm up thoroughly and improves their skills at the same time.

Figure of 8 sprint

Objectives

To enable children to:
- increase their heart rate
- work in larger groups
- experience and practise a change of pace.

Resources and class management

Children work in groups of four.

What to do

Tell the children to find a partner, then to stand with another pair making a group of four. Ask each group to organize themselves so that they are standing one behind another facing a space ahead of the front child. The leading child of each group should move slowly, making a figure of 8 pattern and using up as much of the

available space as possible. Tell the remaining three children in each group that they must follow behind the leader, but must also keep their place in the line at all times. Point out to the children that they must not let gaps develop between themselves and the runner in front. Allow the first child to lead for a short time, then blow a whistle or shout the command 'Go!'. On this command the fourth runner should sprint from behind the group past the remaining three children to the front and become the lead runner. Continue with this until all of the children have had a turn at sprinting from behind to the front, or until the children are well warmed up.

Differentiation
In order to make this task easier, children could work in pairs instead of groups of four. With very young children it is a good idea to ask them to face you and watch while you trace the shape of a large figure 8 in the air as a demonstration. They should then try this themselves, making sure that they do a figure of 8 as large as possible so that they are doing a warming-up activity at the same time.

Now or later
When the children have done this activity on a number of occasions, make the size of the groups much larger, for example working in groups of eight instead of four. By doing this the children have to sprint faster for longer when taking their place at the front of the group, and it allows the children to co-operate in much larger groups. Whilst this may take practice, it is an excellent introduction to the playing of team games at a later stage.

Cross-curricular links
Maths
Recognizing simple spatial patterns and relationships.

PSHE
Listening to other people and working co-operatively.

Whistle stop

Resources and class management
Children work as individuals for this activity. You will need a whistle.

What to do
Ask the children to find a space and stand in it facing in any direction, but with some space in front of them. Tell them that when you blow your whistle, you want them to start running, and that they should keep running at their own speed until they hear the whistle again. Allow time for the children to move around before blowing the whistle. At the sound of the second whistle they must stop as quickly as possible and stand absolutely still, remaining so until they hear the whistle again, when they should resume running. Tell the children that whilst it is tempting to run very slowly in order to stop quickly, they must run at a reasonable speed in order to practise the

Objectives
To enable children to:
- follow instructions whilst moving
- increase the heart rate
- change direction at speed.

Cross-curricular links
Music
Listening with concentration.

Gymnastics
Varying speed and direction.

technique. Make sure that you do not keep the children running for too long before blowing the whistle for them to stop – this is intended to be a short activity to get children listening and moving.

Differentiation

If you are introducing this activity near the very beginning of the lesson on a day when the air temperature is low, it is a good idea to start by having the children walk quickly instead of running, as this ensures that leg muscles are properly warmed-up before attempting something faster.

With very young children who have difficulty sustaining running for any length of time, this activity should be practised regularly so that children build up to a time when they can run for several minutes before stopping.

Now or later

When the children are very familiar with this activity, you can vary the commands that the children follow when the whistle is blown. For example, instead of stopping still on the whistle, tell the children to change direction as fast as they can and begin running again, choosing a new direction each time the whistle is blown. This is a good activity to increase agility of footwork and can be used as a good introduction to any activity that relies on the skill of dodging.

Rolling rings

Objectives

To enable children to:
- practise an underarm bowling technique
- to warm up their hand-eye co-ordination
- to work with a partner.

Cross-curricular links

Dance
Responding to a range of stimuli.

Resources and class management

Children work in pairs. Each pair will need one quoit between them.

What to do

Ask the children to find a partner and collect one quoit between them before moving into a space. Tell pairs to stand facing each other about seven or eight paces apart.

Ask those children with the quoit to hold it in one hand, gripping it with the quoit pointing towards the ground. Right-handed children should have their right foot behind their body; left-handed children should have their left foot back. They should bend both knees and, at the same time, swing the arm holding the quoit back as far as they can. Keeping their knees bent, they should bring their arm forward and release the quoit along the ground towards their partner, who should try to catch it as it arrives and then return it in the same way.

Differentiation

It is not easy to make the quoits roll, and children may need to practise the technique on their own before trying it with a partner. Ask the children to practise releasing the quoit at different stages of swinging the arm forward: they will be able to see what a difference it makes getting the right moment for release. Younger children could begin by holding the quoit as described but throwing it in the air to a partner before attempting to roll it along the ground.

Now or later

Ask the children to collect one quoit each if there is enough equipment, or split the children into groups and have one group of children working at a time while the others observe. Tell the children to form a line side by side and face in one direction. Ask them to swing their arm and release the quoit as before, but this time to aim to roll the quoit as far as possible along the ground. Encourage the children to watch their quoit carefully, see where it stops rolling and to try to improve on their own efforts next time. This can be followed by telling the children to return to working with their partner, but this time substantially increasing the distance between them. It is a good idea when rolling longer distances to line all the pairs up facing in the same direction, so that children running after quoits which have gone astray will not be in danger of bumping into others.

Quoit throw

Resources and class management

Children work in pairs. Each pair will need one beanbag and two quoits. You will need a stopwatch or timer.

What to do

Ask the children to find a partner and to collect one quoit each and one beanbag between them. Tell them to find themselves a space and place the beanbag on the ground in front of them. They should then move away from the beanbag. Younger children will need to be quite close to the beanbag (approximately three paces away), but older or more able children can move up to seven or eight paces away.

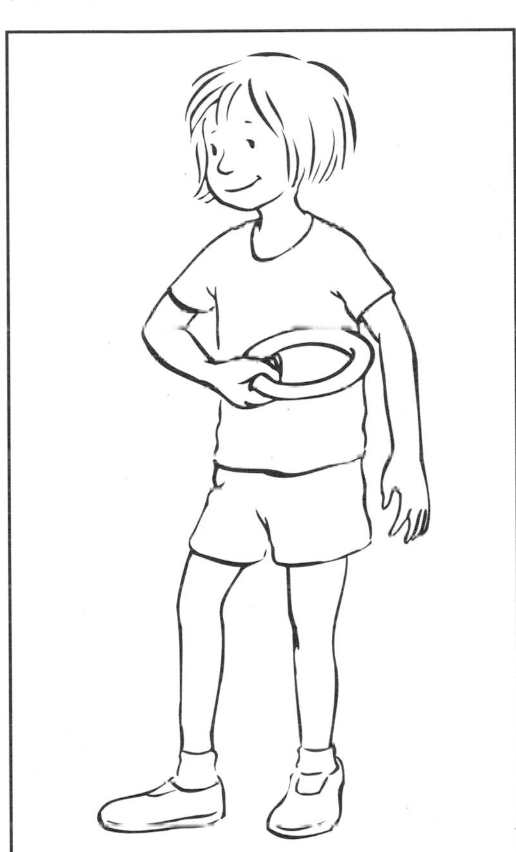

Show the children how to grasp their quoit with one hand and lift it so that the open circle of the quoit is horizontal. Bend the wrist inwards so that it draws the quoit towards the stomach then, using a sharp outward flick away from the body, the quoit should be propelled towards the beanbag. Tell the children that they should aim to make the quoit land over the beanbag. The children will need plenty of practice at this, but when they become more confident introduce the idea that they keep score as they play. Score one point every time they manage to throw the quoit successfully over the beanbag in a set time of, say, one minute. Keep a record and see if children can beat their own best score on another occasion.

Differentiation

Older or more able children could see if they can throw the quoit over a skittle.

Younger children could try replacing the beanbag with a hoop and try to throw the quoit so that it lands inside the hoop instead of making it land over the beanbag.

Now or later

As this is a warming-up activity, it is a good idea to always start with the easier version introduced in 'Differentiation' above so that children can work on their hand-eye co-ordination. When children have had plenty of practice at this activity and their aim is improving, adjust the task to make it more difficult. Place the beanbag on the ground as before, and ask the children to stand further away from and to the side of it. They should run towards the beanbag and, as they pass to the left or right of it, they should try and throw their quoit over the beanbag. If several children are using the same beanbag, remind them to take care when running, and to let everyone in their group have a turn before retrieving the quoits.

Objectives

To enable children to:
- practise aiming at a distant object
- learn an alternative way to throw a quoit
- warm up shoulder muscles and joints.

Cross-curricular links

Dance

Changing the rhythm, speed, level and direction of movements.

Invasion games
Skills for one or two players

The activities in this section cover tasks and skills relevant in hockey, netball and football. As these are considered to be 'major' games, the skills and group activities associated with them need to be practised regularly throughout the autumn and spring terms. The activities in Section 2a focus on skills for one or two children; those in Section 2b on activities for three or more children.

Photocopiable page 55 ('My progress chart') can be used when back in the classroom at the end of a games lesson as a means of recording the children's progress. You may wish to use discretion as to whether to chart progress after every lesson or only occasionally during the term. The information on the recording sheets will be useful for assessment come the end of a term of work.

The activities in this section focus on

- practising the skills of dribbling, kicking, throwing and bouncing
- using the space to feint and dodge away from a partner
- working co-operatively with other children
- using a variety of equipment
- using different parts of the body
- practising aiming skills.

Kick, stop, kick

Objectives
To enable children to:
- practise kicking skills
- practise trapping skills
- practise accurate passing.

Cross-curricular links
Gymnastics
Performing basic skills in travelling, being still, finding space and using it safely.

Resources and class management
Children work in pairs. Each pair will need one large ball between them.

What to do
Tell the children to find a partner and to face one another with seven or eight paces between them. To avoid any collisions, make sure each pair of children is facing in roughly the same direction. Tell the children holding the ball to put it on the ground in front of them. They should then take a few paces back, run towards the ball and, watching the ball carefully, should turn their right or left foot (whichever feels most comfortable to them; at this level, using either foot will not affect the activity) slightly to the side and kick the ball using the inside of the foot near the toes (the body will also turn slightly to the preferred side). Emphasize that the point of this exercise is to get the ball to their partner accurately, and without using too much force. After they have kicked the ball it will be necessary to run a few more steps so that they do not stop very suddenly or in a jerky manner which may cause damage to joints.

The children who are receiving should watch the ball carefully on its journey towards them, and as it arrives in front of them should 'trap' the ball by lightly placing their preferred foot on it. Once they have stopped the ball successfully, they should swing their leg back, kicking the ball back to their partner as before. The partner traps and stops the ball, then returns it with a kick, this time omitting the run-up. The pairs should continue passing the ball between each other until they can consistently trap the ball and return it to their partner with confidence.

If the children are not very accurate with their passing at the beginning of the lesson, encourage them to move towards the ball as they see it coming from their partner.

Differentiation
It is important for very young children to use as large a ball as possible (for example, a rubber ball the size of a football), and to keep the distance between themselves

and their partner as short as necessary, say just four or five paces apart.

Older or more able children should be encouraged to keep the flow of movement between them going without interruption.

Now or later

As the children improve at this task they should be encouraged to aim the ball towards one side of their partner rather than directly at them. The children receiving should anticipate where the ball will arrive and move towards that spot to trap the ball and return it. As the children improve further, tell them to kick the ball to their partner's non-preferred side for some turns so that experience is gained in using both sides of the body.

Feint and dodge

Objectives

To enable children to:

- use space skilfully
- lose a partner who is marking them
- learn the skill of feinting.

Resources and class management

Children work in pairs. Each pair will need to have a space in which to practise that is large enough to enable them to run in any direction.

What to do

Tell the children to find a partner, label themselves 'A' and 'B', and to stand in a space facing each other, standing one large stride apart. 'A' stands with their feet slightly apart and, leaning slightly to one side, runs sideways in that direction for two or three steps and stops quickly. Then, leaning in the other direction with their body, 'A' runs quickly in that direction as before, stops quickly, and this time sets off much faster in the opposite direction with the intention of leaving his or her partner behind. During this time, 'B' should try and follow their partner's movements and keep level with 'A'. Make sure the children know that they should run quite short distances in each direction when they are trying to lose their partner, and suggest that they run several times in each direction in order to try and confuse their partner, gaining ground more easily. Finally, make sure the children who are following realize that they should always be looking at their partner in order to judge when to make the final last short sprint. The aim is for 'B' to keep up with their partner's movements and remain facing them as they move to one side or the other.

Differentiation

If very young children find this activity difficult, give them a sequence to copy, for example run right, run left, run right, sprint left. Even if they do not lose their partner they will be gaining the early skills of 'feint and dodge'.

Older or more able children could be encouraged to use the top part of their body to try to put off their partner as well as running: tell the children to move the top of their body quickly to the left then right, then left again before sprinting to the right.

Now or later

When children are regularly losing their partner without too much hard running, they could be taught to signal to an imaginary player that they are ready to receive a 'pass'. Tell the children that when they are sure they are several paces free of their partner they should raise one hand and arm straight in the air to signal to imaginary team players. If they are moving to the right, the right hand should be raised, and if moving to the left the left hand should be raised. This will prepare the children for later work on playing mini-games (see Section 5).

Long and short throwing

Objectives

To enable children to:

- practise overarm throwing
- practise accurate throwing
- use different levels of force.

Cross-curricular links

Science

Finding out about, and describing the movement of familiar things.

Resources and class management

Children work in pairs. Each pair will need one large ball between them.

What to do

Ask the children, in their pairs, to stand facing each other with a short distance between them. Give one child in each pair a ball.

The child who has the ball should stand with it in both hands at shoulder-height on their preferred side, with the same foot back. The top part of the body should be turned slightly towards the preferred side, one hand should be behind the ball, and the other hand should be in front of the ball supporting it. Tell the children with the ball to transfer their body weight to their back foot and to push the ball hard towards their partner, aiming it in a straight line. As the ball leaves their hands, their body weight should be transferred forwards to assist the ball in its flight and to give power to the throw.

Encourage the children who are receiving the ball to reach out with their hands and arms, and as they receive the ball to pull it towards the middle of their body before moving it in a fluid movement round to their preferred shoulder ready for a return throw. Tell the children to pass the ball between them like this twice more, then to move slightly further away from each other and repeat the throwing twice more. Then they should move slightly further away again, so that they are throwing longer and longer distances each time.

If the children are having difficulty throwing the ball accurately to their partner, tell them that if they look at their partner as they throw the ball they will achieve greater accuracy.

Differentiation

When children first learn this activity, it is a good idea to keep the same distance between pairs as they throw and to increase the distance gradually. Very young children can use balls that are somewhere between tennis ball and football size; the younger the child, the larger the ball. It may be a good idea for the very youngest children to use sponge balls for safety.

Encourage older or more able children to keep the fluidity of the movement going. Even if the ball is dropped, children should be encouraged to retrieve it quickly and return it immediately.

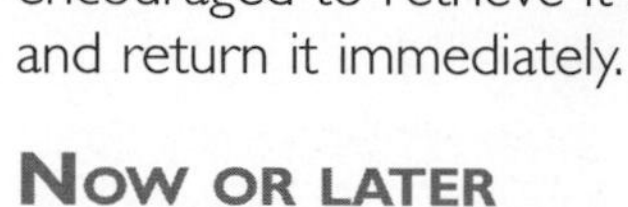

Now or later

When the children have mastered throwing and catching successfully, ask them to count the number of successful throws they can complete in a set time and to try and beat their own record on another occasion.

FIGURE OF 8 DRIBBLE

RESOURCES AND CLASS MANAGEMENT

Children work independently. Each child will need one large or medium-sized ball. You will need a whistle.

WHAT TO DO

Tell the children to stand with some free space immediately in front of them, and to put their ball on the ground by their feet. Ask them to raise a hand in the air and draw the shape of the number 8 in front of them. (With very young children, this can be repeated several times.) Next, ask them to walk the shape of the number 8 around the balls that are on the ground – this will give them a good idea of the shape they will be making when they dribble the ball.

When you are confident that they can do this easily, tell the children to lightly tap the ball ahead of them using the top or inside of their preferred foot, and to follow the ball. As the ball slows, they should tap the ball with the other foot and then run to follow it. Encourage the children to keep the ball close to their feet. As they continue dribbling the ball forwards they should be making the shape of the number 8 on the ground as they run.

When the children have practised this, tell them that when you blow a whistle or shout a command they should run faster and move the ball quicker until they hear the next whistle, when they should slow down again.

DIFFERENTIATION

Very young children could practise this activity using the shape of a square or a circle, or a shape that is more familiar to them.

Older or more able children could be encouraged to use the same foot to tap the ball forward each time, and could be encouraged to change speed in their own time.

NOW OR LATER

When children become familiar with this practice, you could set out obstacles such as cones to dribble around, or use other children who stand still whilst those with a ball dribble around them.

OBJECTIVES

To enable children to:

- practise the skill of dribbling the ball
- use the space in a structured way
- experience changes of speed.

CROSS-CURRICULAR LINKS

MATHS

Being familiar with numbers.

PSHE

Setting simple goals.

PUSH THE BALL

RESOURCES AND CLASS MANAGEMENT

Children work individually (if you have enough equipment). Young children will need medium-sized balls and older children will need smaller balls (such as tennis balls or rubber balls of a similar size). Each child will need a hockey stick or shinty stick. You will also need some obstacles for the 'Now or later' activity.

WHAT TO DO

If children are new to using a hockey or shinty stick, tell them to place their left hand at the top of the stick and their right hand about halfway down the stick, which should then be placed at the right side of the body and slightly forward. The ball should be placed on the ground in front of the stick. Tell the children to gently swing the stick back and to lightly push the ball

OBJECTIVES

To enable children to:

- handle a stick or a bat
- practise manoeuvring a ball
- use the space available.

ahead of their body. As the ball moves away from them, tell the children to follow it, and to continue to push the ball forward as it slows down. Discourage them from pushing the ball too hard then having to run after the ball – the emphasis should be on control all the time; at this stage the children should only be walking and pushing the ball.

Differentiation

As children become more familiar with this practice, or for those who are older or more able, encourage them to begin to increase their speed as they push the ball ahead of their body, but continue to encourage control at all times.

Now or later

As children become proficient at pushing the ball and increasing their speed, obstacles can be set out in a variety of patterns on the playground or field and children can practise guiding the ball around the obstacles. Tell the children that it is necessary to keep their feet moving all the time as they weave in and out of the obstacles. This should place the body in the correct position for pushing the ball in the right direction.

Alternate bounce

Objectives

To enable children to:
- practise the skill of bouncing a ball
- improve skill using both hands
- build up a sequence of movements.

Cross-curricular links

Gymnastics
Creating and performing short, linked sequences.

Mathematics
Counting reliably up to 20.

Resources and class management

Children work independently. Each child will need one large ball each. This activity is best practised on a hard surface such as a playground or the school hall.

What to do

Tell the children that they are going to practise bouncing a ball on the ground using both their right and left hands. Ask them to hold the ball in their preferred hand with their fingers spread over the top of the ball, then push it hard towards the ground, trying to keep the ball as close to their feet as possible. Younger children may need to hold the ball with both hands to begin, then let go with one hand as they push the ball downwards.

As the ball bounces upwards tell the children to push it down again using the same hand, keeping the hand flat with fingers spread. Ask them to count the number of bounces they can do without stopping or losing control of the ball. Tell them they may move their feet to keep bouncing the ball, but each time the ball is only allowed to bounce once before they should bounce it back down. When they have practised this and are becoming more confident with their preferred hand, tell them to try repeating the skill but using the other hand. Finally, let the children try and bounce the ball with alternate hands so that they use the sequence left, right, left, right, or right, left, right, left.

Differentiation

Very young children can begin to learn this skill at first by bouncing the ball on the ground using both hands, holding it at each side.

Older or more able children can be encouraged to try and keep the bouncing pattern going without having to move their feet at all.

Now or later

As the children become proficient at this practice, encourage them to bounce the ball faster. This can be done in two ways: pushing the ball down harder towards the ground so it returns more quickly, or bouncing the ball back down before it bounces up to waist height.

Finally, let the children make up sequence patterns when bouncing the ball, such as three bounces with right hand, followed by three bounces with left hand; two bounces with each hand, then one bounce with each hand.

Invasion games
Group activities for three players or more

The activities in this part focus on:
- building teamwork skills
- using relay techniques
- introducing a competitive element
- using space in a variety of ways
- practising ball throwing, rolling and shooting skills
- practising dodging and marking techniques.

Count and throw

Objectives

To enable children to:
- work co-operatively in a small group
- practise underarm throwing
- practise throwing at increased speed.

Resources and class management

Children work in groups of four. Each group will need one beanbag. You will also need a whistle and a stopwatch.

What to do

Ask the children to form into groups of four, and give one child in each group a beanbag. In their fours the children should form a circle by holding hands and stretching their arms out straight. Tell them to release their hands but to keep their position, as this will be the distance they will need to throw: they are going to throw the beanbag to every person in the circle in turn, and at the same time count the number of throws. Tell the child with the beanbag in each group to turn towards the person on their left and, with their right hand and right foot back (or left hand and left foot back if preferred), they must swing their arm back before releasing the beanbag underarm to the person on their left. As the beanbag is released the child calls out the number 1. The child receiving the beanbag may catch it with one or two hands (whichever is easiest), transfer it to their preferred hand and, turning to their left, throw it underarm as before, calling out the number 2 as they do so. This continues around the circle with each child calling out the next number until you blow a whistle or call out the command 'Stop!'

Differentiation

If using this practice with very young children you could call out the numbers for them. Tell them that they should throw each time you call out a number.

Older or more able children could try throwing the beanbag to anyone in the circle, rather than moving the beanbag in sequence around the circle. Impress upon the children the need for alertness if they are throwing to anyone in the circle.

Now or later

When the children have practised this a number of times, tell them that you are going to time them and see how many throws they can make in two minutes.

Piggy in the middle roll

Objectives

To enable children to:

- practise the skill of rolling a ball
- practise intercepting a ball
- improve accuracy techniques.

Cross-curricular links

PSHE

Playing and working co-operatively.

Resources and class management

Children work in groups of three. Each group will need one large ball.

What to do

Tell the children to form groups of three and to collect one ball between the group. Tell them that they are going to play 'piggy in the middle roll'.

Ask the children to stand in a line, with one of the end players holding a ball and facing the middle person about 6 or 7 strides away. The third player should be

standing a further 6 or 7 paces behind the middle person and should be facing his/her back. The player with the ball stands with it held on their preferred side, with the same foot behind their body. Tell them that they should bend their knees, swing the ball back on their preferred side, then release the ball along the ground to the right- or left-hand side of the player in the middle. The middle player should watch the ball as it approaches them and try and intercept the ball. If they fail to intercept the ball the player at the other end should be ready to bend down low and, reaching forward with their hands, retrieve the ball from the ground.

If the middle player successfully intercepts the ball then that person changes places with the player who rolled the ball and repeats the rolling movement. If the ball reaches its target, the player receiving it at the other end should hold the ball to one side and repeat the rolling action, trying to get the ball to the player at the other end. When the children have played for a while, check with them that everyone has had a turn at rolling and intercepting the ball.

Differentiation

Very young children can practise rolling the ball in pairs before they try with the third person in the middle. Even so, encourage them to roll the ball to one side of their partner so that the second child gets used to moving their feet in order to retrieve the ball.

Encourage older or more able children to increase the speed of the rolling ball by swinging their arm back faster before releasing.

Now or later

As a development of this activity, the middle player could try standing directly in front of the player trying to receive the ball. Tell the player receiving the ball to dodge to one side or the other and the player with the ball should roll the ball towards the dodging player at an appropriate moment.

Two versus two

Objectives

To enable children to:

- practise overarm throwing
- improve technique of feinting and dodging
- practise silent signalling.

Resources and class management

Children work in groups of four. Each group will need one large ball.

What to do

Tell the children this is a competitive activity, with two pairs playing against one another, focusing on throwing a ball and getting free from a marker.

Tell the children to form groups of four, and to each choose a partner to play with; each two children will form a team. Give one of the players in each group of four a ball. Tell them that they should try to wait until their partner is free from their marker before throwing an overarm throw to that person. The other pair will be the 'markers', and should each pick one person to mark and try and intercept the ball as it is thrown to them.

Tell those children who are marking the receiver that they should try and stay in front of that person wherever they move, but should also be facing the player with the ball so that they know when it is thrown; the children who are being marked should keep their feet still but move the top half of their body quickly to the left then the right before sprinting away from their marker. As they leave their marker behind, encourage them to raise a hand high to signal to the player with the ball that they are free to receive it. When the player with the ball sees the signal they must throw the ball with their preferred hand (with the corresponding foot back) from shoulder height to the player who is signalling. This can continue in the same way, with the person who threw the ball now becoming the receiver. If the ball is intercepted by one of the other players, they then become thrower, their partner becomes receiver, and the other two become markers.

If the practice becomes one-sided, with one of the pairs keeping the ball a long time, then stop the group and ask the players with the ball to give it to the other players in their group.

Differentiation

Younger children can practise this activity without using the signalling method, and it may be necessary to tell the children to give the ball to the other side after each turn at throwing.

Older or more able children should be encouraged to feint and dodge in the smallest possible space and should be discouraged from using natural speed to run away from their marker.

Now or later

When children are familiar with this activity, you can change the type of throw that is used and introduce a chest pass, bounce pass or overhead pass – either using one for each session, or letting the children use a variety according to the circumstances (for example, if the distance is small between thrower and receiver a chest pass will be appropriate, but if the receiver is having trouble getting free from their marker, a bounce pass to one side of the receiver may be more appropriate).

SHUTTLE RELAY

OBJECTIVES
To enable children to:
- experience a competitive team game
- improve accuracy of passing and receiving
- improve general fitness levels.

CROSS-CURRICULAR LINKS
PSHE
Agreeing and following rules for a group.

SCIENCE
Taking exercise helps humans to keep healthy.

RESOURCES AND CLASS MANAGEMENT
Children work in groups of six. Each group will need one small tennis or rubber ball. Hockey sticks are needed for extending the activity. You will need to carry out this activity in a large open space, such as the playground or school hall.

WHAT TO DO
Tell the children that they are going to split their group of six into two groups of three children each. One group of three should stand one behind the other at one end of the playground, field or hall, with the front child holding the ball. The other group of three children in the same group should go to the opposite end of the playground and stand one behind the other facing the other half of their team. Tell the children they are going to play a team race, and the winning team will be the group of six children who finish in their original positions first.

Tell the children that when you shout 'Go!' the players with the ball must run as fast as they can towards their team-mates at the other end of the playground. On reaching the other end they should hand the ball to the leader whilst still moving, and then run to the back of that group. As soon as the receiving child has the ball in their hands they should begin running quickly towards the waiting group at the other end of the playground and repeat the handing over of the ball as before. Encourage the children receiving the ball to hold out cupped hands as soon as the runner with the ball is within reach. This continues until all the children have received the ball and run with it and are standing back in their original positions.

DIFFERENTIATION
Younger children should have only ten or twelve paces between each group, and should begin this practice with only four children – two at each end. They may also use a larger ball which makes the hand-over easier to manage.

Now or later

- To allow children to experience this activity in a variety of ways, try letting the children use larger balls and dribble the ball to the other half of their group.
- Groups could also try dribbling the ball with hockey sticks, but in this case it will be necessary for two children in each group to have a hockey stick, passing it forward to the child receiving the ball.

Beanbag sprint

Objectives

To enable children to:

- practise aiming techniques
- improve general fitness
- practise in a team situation.

Cross-curricular links

Dance

Changing the speed and direction of movement.

Resources and class management

Children work in groups of four. Each team will need one container or hoop and a beanbag for each child. This activity needs to be carried out in a large space, such as the school playground or field.

What to do

Tell the children they are going to race as a team against the other teams; the object being to place all the beanbags in their container and to return to their original places.

Tell the children to form into groups of four, and to collect one beanbag for each child and a container for each team. They should place their containers at one end of the playground in a line, with several paces between each one. Ask the children to move to the other end of the playground and stand in their teams, one behind another and facing their container. On your command, the first person in each team must run as fast as possible towards their container and throw or drop their beanbag into it before running back to join their team at the back of the line. As they return, tell them to touch the arm of the new leader, which is a signal to that person to begin running towards the container as before. Finally, tell the children that the winning team will be the team who have put all their beanbags in the container and returned to their original positions before raising a hand to signal they have completed the task.

Differentiation

Younger children may need a larger container, such as a bucket, which will enable them to throw or drop the beanbag in more easily.

Older children can be given a small hoop in which to put their beanbags, which will encourage greater accuracy.

Now or later

When children are familiar with this activity you could exchange the container for a target such as a skittle and tell the children to throw their beanbag at the skittle as they run past to try to knock it over. Tell them to wait until they are in front of the skittle and about four paces away from it before throwing. If the children are not successful with a beanbag, it could be substituted with a small rubber ball.

Shoot and hit

Objectives

To enable children to:

- practise aiming at a target
- practise overarm throwing
- practise retrieving a ball.

Cross-curricular links

Gymnastics

Choosing and linking skills and actions in short movement phrases.

Mathematics

Recognizing movements in a straight line.

Resources and class management

Children work in groups of three. Each group will need one large or medium-sized ball and one skittle or piece of equipment suitable as a target. You will need photocopiable page 57 ('Name the equipment') for 'Now or later'.

What to do

Tell the children to form groups of three, and to collect one ball and one skittle between each group. Ask them to place the skittle upright on the ground. The child in each group with the ball should stand facing the skittle five or six paces away from it; one of the other two children should stand behind the skittle, facing the player with the ball, and the remaining child in each group should stand behind the player with the ball.

Tell the children that the child with the ball in each group is going to throw the ball underarm at the skittle to try to knock it over. The child standing behind the skittle should retrieve the ball and return it with an overarm throw to the child waiting behind the first player, who should aim at the skittle again with an underarm throw. They should re-set the skittle if it has been knocked down. After the first child has aimed at the skittle, they should stand behind the player who will throw the ball next.

After the children have practised this a number of times, ask them to change places so that everyone gets a chance to retrieve the ball and return it overarm to the receiver. Remind the children that right-handed throwers should have their right leg behind them and left-handed throwers should have their left leg behind them.

Differentiation

Younger children should be given a larger ball and as big a target as possible. Older or more able children should be given smaller balls and smaller targets.

Now or later

When the children can do this activity with a good degree of accuracy, tell them to aim at the target as soon as they have received the ball from the retriever. Equally, encourage the retriever to gather up the ball from the ground and, in one fluid movement, place the feet in the correct position to return the ball immediately to the receiver. Encourage speed and accuracy throughout the activity.

Photocopiable page 57 ('Name the equipment') can be used back in the classroom to reinforce learning about the new types of PE equipment introduced during this lesson.

Striking and fielding games
Skills for one or two players

Striking and fielding games cover all forms of rounders and tennis activities, and therefore should ideally be practised during the summer term. Many schools will have the use of a field during this term, and providing the weather is suitable most of these activities can take place on a field. If the weather is inclement, though, the activities can easily be adapted for play on a playground or in the hall.

Each activity will give suggestions for distances between players as they practise skills. When you know your children well, these distances can be adjusted where necessary to make the activities more challenging where appropriate, or to make the activities more achievable for less able children or those with physical disabilities.

Photocopiable page 59 ('What can I do?' chart) can be used by the children as they work through the activities to reinforce vocabulary and allow them opportunities to plot their own development.

The activities in this section focus on:

- practising the skills of throwing, catching, hitting and bowling
- giving opportunities for aiming at targets
- learning to retrieve a ball
- co-operating in small groups
- using a variety of equipment
- encouraging spatial awareness.

Wall bounce

Resources and class management

Children will work individually. Each child will need a tennis ball or a small rubber ball. You will need a high wall for this activity.

Objectives

To enable children to:

- practise underarm throwing
- practise retrieving a ball
- practise aiming skills.

What to do

Tell the children to collect a ball each and stand facing the wall approximately four paces away from it. Tell them that they are going to throw the ball underarm to a point on the wall slightly above head height, then let it rebound and bounce once before catching it. The children should hold the ball in their preferred hand and swing the arm back behind the body, at the same time placing the same leg and foot back. Swinging the arm forward, they should release the ball as their arm approaches shoulder height, bringing their body weight forward on to the front foot as they do so. Remind them to watch the ball carefully, and when it has rebounded from the wall to let it bounce once before reaching forward with both hands cupped and fingers spread ready to catch the ball. Warn the children that, because the ball may bounce quickly off the wall, they will need to be ready to move in to position in order to move to the ball and retrieve it.

Differentiation

Younger children can begin with a larger ball and use both hands to throw it towards the wall. Younger children could also try swinging their arm back more slowly so that the speed of the ball will be slower and it will be easier to catch the rebound. Likewise, very able children could be encouraged to speed up the swing of their arm to increase the speed of the ball and thus the speed of their reactions.

Now or later

When the children are familiar with this practice, you can increase the distance between the children and the wall. They could also try experimenting with the height at which the ball is released, asking them to notice what happens to the bounce when the ball hits the wall at a greater height: they may have to run backwards to retrieve the ball as it bounces further away from the wall. When teaching children this part of the activity, make sure that they turn their body sideways before they run backwards, or that they turn completely and run forwards to collect the ball.

Two throw quoits

Objectives

To enable children to:
- practise underarm throwing with a quoit
- practise catching and retrieving skills
- improve aiming techniques.

Resources and class management

Children work in pairs. Each child will need a quoit.

What to do

Give each child a quoit, ask them to form pairs, and tell them that they are going to throw and catch their two quoits at the same time. They should stand facing each other, approximately six paces apart, holding the quoit in their preferred hand at the side of the body, with their arm straight and leg and foot on that side of the body behind them. Each child should shout '1... 2... 3... Go!', and swing back the arm holding the quoit, then swing it forward and at the same time transfer their weight onto the front foot. The quoit should be released as it reaches shoulder height, and the children must be prepared to catch their partner's quoit as soon as they have thrown their own. This should be done by reaching forward with outstretched arms, and as the quoit is caught it should be pulled towards the chest or stomach area. If the quoit is not caught tell the children that they should run and pick it up before returning to their places, calling out '1... 2... 3... Go!' again and repeating the practice.

Differentiation

Younger children may find it easier to begin this practice using beanbags, then moving on to quoits when they are more confident.

With older or more able children emphasize the need to co-ordinate the command of '1... 2... 3... Go!' so that the throwing really is simultaneous.

Now or later

Older or more able children can replace the quoits with tennis balls, rubber balls, or medium-sized balls when they have gained some degree of skill. You can then choose whether to let them throw the ball with one hand in the same way as the quoit, or whether to let them throw slightly larger balls with two hands.

HOOP BOUNCE

RESOURCES AND CLASS MANAGEMENT

Children work in pairs. Each pair will need one large ball and one large hoop between them. You will need a stopwatch with a second hand on it.

WHAT TO DO

Ask the children to form pairs and collect one large ball and one hoop between them, placing the hoop flat on the ground. Tell them that they are going to bounce the ball to each other, trying to make it bounce inside the large hoop before it is caught. Each child in the pair should stand on opposite sides of the hoop, walk five paces away from it, then turn to face their partner: they will now be standing opposite one another, with the hoop halfway between them. Tell the child with the ball that they should hold it in both hands at chest height, with one foot back behind their body and their body weight on the back foot. They should push the ball hard towards the ground, aiming for the centre of the hoop, at the same time moving their body weight forward onto the front foot. Their partner, who will be receiving the ball, should stretch out their arms with fingers spread to catch the ball, then bring it towards their chest before repeating the bounce back to their partner, again aiming to bounce the ball into the centre of the hoop. Finally, tell the children that they are allowed to move their feet if necessary in order to catch or retrieve the ball.

DIFFERENTIATION

Younger children who have difficulty in bouncing the ball inside the hoop can begin the activity nearer to the hoop, say only three paces away from it.

Older or more able children can gradually move further away from the hoop and see how far back they can go, whilst still maintaining accurate bouncing and catching.

NOW OR LATER

Encourage the children to build up a fluidity of movement by bouncing, catching, and returning the ball immediately, in order to keep the ball moving all the time. Children will enjoy counting the number of times they can do this without dropping the ball, or the number of times they can perform the this sequence in two minutes.

OBJECTIVES

To enable children to:
- practise aiming skills
- practise the technique of bouncing a ball
- practise catching and retrieving a ball.

CROSS-CURRICULAR LINKS

GYMNASTICS
Linking skills and actions in short movement phrases.

RUN AND RETRIEVE

RESOURCES AND CLASS MANAGEMENT

Children work in pairs; each pair will need a small ball. This activity is best practised on grass, as a hard surface makes the ball move too quickly for younger children. You will also need photocopiable page 58 ('Find the mistakes') for 'Now or later'.

WHAT TO DO

Tell the children to find a space and stand diagonally to their partner, at least ten paces apart. The child with the ball in each pair should roll it along the ground across the pathway of their partner, so that the other child can run forward and collect the

OBJECTIVES

To enable children to:
- retrieve a moving ball
- practise rolling techniques
- work co-operatively.

Cross-curricular links
Gymnastics
Performing basic skills in travelling, finding a space and using it safely.

ball. Remind the children holding the ball that they should swing back the arm holding the ball, at the same time placing the leg on that side of their body behind them, with their weight on the back foot. As they swing their arm forward to roll the ball, tell them to bend the front leg and lean their body forwards, releasing the ball close to the ground. After the ball has been released, tell the children retrieving it to run quickly towards the path of the ball and reach forward and downwards with their arms and hands outstretched to pick up the ball. Making sure they are again standing diagonally to their partner, the retriever repeats the rolling process, with their partner collecting the ball in the same way as before. Finally, tell the children that when they have collected the ball, they should try and keep moving and try to get themselves into the correct position to repeat the movement, rather than just picking up the ball and standing still.

Differentiation
Younger children can practise with a larger ball so that it rolls more slowly, enabling the other child to retrieve it more easily. Older children can be encouraged to move further away from their partner, and so run further before retrieving the ball.

Now or later
■ When the children are familiar with this practice, they can try using an overarm throw to return the ball to their partner once they have retrieved the ball. This will involve them moving the feet and body into the correct position for an overarm throw – that is, with the right hand and right foot back or left hand and left foot back depending on preference. After several attempts, tell the children to change their roles so that they experience both rolling and retrieving.
■ To reinforce learning about safety, you may wish to ask children to complete photocopiable page 58 ('Find the mistakes') in the classroom after the lesson. The answers for page 58 are: 1. The child's T-shirt has one longer sleeve; 2. He has the wrong foot forward for the hand he is holding the ball in; 3. He is wearing only one sock; 4. He is wearing ordinary school shoes rather than plimsolls; 5. He is wearing a watch on his left wrist; 6. His shorts are longer on one leg than the other.

Bowl and bounce

Objectives
To enable children to:
- pass and return a pass with different throws
- practise bowling underarm
- practise a bounce pass.

Cross-curricular links
Gymnastics
Linking skills and actions in short movement phrases.

Resources and class management
Children work in pairs. Each pair will need a small tennis or rubber ball which will easily bounce. This activity is best practised on a hard surface, such as a playground or a hall, but if the school field is very dry and hard, it could also be used.

What to do
Tell the children they are going to pass the ball to each other, alternately throwing underarm and bouncing it between them. Tell them to stand facing their partner approximately eight paces away from one another. The child with the ball should aim an underarm throw to their partner. They should swing back the arm holding the ball, and at the same time place the leg on the same side back with their body weight resting on it. Swinging the arm forward, and transferring their body weight on to the front foot, tell them to release the ball towards their partner when the arm and

hand reach approximately shoulder height. Those who are receiving the ball should stretch out their arms with fingers spread and, as they catch the ball, pull it into their body level with their waist and lower chest. Transferring the ball to their preferred side, ask them to put the leg on the same side of the body behind them; their hands should be cupped around the ball, and they should push it hard towards the ground at a spot approximately halfway between themselves and their partner, who should aim to collect the ball. The children receiving the bounce pass should watch the ball from the time it is released until they catch it. Repeat this sequence several times, before asking the children to swap over so that they each have a turn at trying both methods of passing the ball.

If the children have difficulty catching the ball, encourage them to keep watching the ball all the time, and to move their feet to retrieve the ball before returning to their throwing position.

Differentiation

Young children who find it difficult to bounce the ball accurately could use a mark made with chalk or tape halfway between themselves and their partner as a guide.

Older or more able children can organize their passing so that they each do a throw and bounce pass without interrupting the flow. For example, tell them to throw underarm, bounce, bounce, throw underarm in that order.

Now or later

When the children have practised this a number of times, encourage them to try and speed up the throwing and catching sequence without dropping the ball, and still retain the accuracy of their passing. Tell them that to achieve this they must swing their arm faster on the underarm throw, and shorten the time it takes to move into position from collecting the ball to the beginning of the bounce pass. If accuracy is sacrificed, go back to the original practice until the children have improved.

Over and under

Resources and class management

Children work in pairs. Each pair will need one small ball between them.

What to do

Tell the children to form pairs, and to collect one ball between each pair; they should stand facing each other with approximately five paces between them. Explain that they are going to pass the ball to each other, first with an underarm pass, followed by an overarm pass, continuing this sequence. Tell the child holding the ball to hold it in their preferred hand, and swing that arm and the leg on the same side of their body back, with their weight on the back foot. The arm should be swung forward underarm and the ball released at just below shoulder height, so that the ball reaches their partner at about waist height. The receiver should reach out with their hands cupped and fingers spread, and as the ball is caught they should bring it into the body at about waist height. If the ball is not caught tell the children to run and pick it up and return to their original starting position.

When the second child has retrieved the ball successfully, tell them to put the ball in their preferred hand, making sure that right-handers have the right foot back and left-handers the left foot back. They should bring the ball up to the appropriate shoulder and throw it overarm from the shoulder in a straight line towards their partner; the body weight should transfer from the back foot to the front foot as they throw. Make sure the children do not throw in the style of a cricket bowling action – the ball should be pushed in a straight line from the shoulder rather than in an arc. Let the children continue with this sequence until they are comfortable with it, then tell them to change over so that they each practise the other type of throw.

Objectives

To enable children to:

- use two different methods of passing a ball
- practise underarm bowling
- practise overarm throwing.

Cross-curricular links

PSHE

Listening to other people; playing and working co-operatively.

Dance

Changing the direction of movement.

Differentiation

Younger or less able children can use a larger ball to make the activity easier.

Reduce or increase the distance between the children according to ability – longer distances for older or more able children, shorter for younger children. However, as one of the throws is an underarm bowling action, it is not a suitable type of throw for a distance greater than about four metres (or four of an adult's strides).

Now or later

This practice can be followed by one in which the children are told to aim the underarm throw slightly to the right or left of their partner, so that the children receiving the ball have to move their feet in order to catch the ball. This is a good introduction to playing mini-games, where the ball rarely arrives in a child's hands without them moving.

Striking and fielding games
Group activities for three players or more

The activities in this section focus on:
- practising the skills of throwing, catching, hitting and bowling
- giving opportunities for aiming at targets
- learning to retrieve a ball
- co-operating in small groups and teamwork
- using a variety of equipment
- encouraging spatial awareness.

Skittle alley

Objectives

To enable children to:
- practise underarm bowling and throwing
- use aiming skills
- practise retrieving skills.

Cross-curricular links

PSHE

Listening to other people; playing and working co-operatively.

Resources and class management

Children work in groups of four. Each group will need one small tennis or rubber ball and three tall skittles or other suitable targets which stand at least thigh-height from the ground.

What to do

Ask the children to form groups of four. Tell each group to collect three skittles and one small ball between them. Tell them to place the skittles close together in a straight line upright on the ground. Explain to the children that within each group one child will be responsible for retrieving the ball, one child will be trying to catch the ball behind the skittles, and two children will be aiming to knock over the skittles. Tell the two children who are aiming to hit the skittles to stand approximately six paces away facing the target – they should have the ball with them. The child who is trying to catch the ball should stand close behind the skittles, facing the two children aiming; the retriever should stand to one side but close to the skittles.

When the children are in position, tell one of the children with the ball to hold the ball in their preferred hand, and put the leg and hand holding the ball behind them, with their weight on the back foot. Swinging the arm and hand forward, they should release the ball underarm at about waist height, aiming to hit the skittles. Make sure that they know that they must transfer their weight forward onto the front foot as the arm is swung forward. As the ball is released, explain that the child behind the skittles should watch the ball carefully to see if they can catch the ball or stop it rolling away as it reaches them, reaching forward with their arms and hands outstretched. Tell the other child retrieving the ball that they must watch the ball carefully too, and if the catcher fails to get the ball they must run and pick it up

before throwing it underarm to the second child who should try again to aim for the skittles. If all the skittles are knocked down at any time, the child collecting the ball should re-set them as before. After several attempts, make sure that the children change positions so that they all have the opportunity to throw and retrieve the ball; this can be done in a formal way so that the children know exactly where they are going. For example, the two children aiming change with the catcher and retriever and rotate in a set order every five throws.

Differentiation

Younger or less able children can try this activity by rolling the ball at the skittles rather than bowling underarm. The retriever may stand behind the catcher, which cuts down the amount of running that may be needed to retrieve the ball. More able children can throw from further away and/or use smaller targets to improve their accuracy.

Now or later

When the children have practised this activity on a number of occasions you can cut the number of skittles down to two, providing they are placed close enough to ensure a reasonable-sized target. Encourage children who are retrieving the ball to collect it as quickly as possible before throwing overarm to the second child aiming the ball.

Beat the ball

Objectives

To enable the children to:

- experience a competitive group activity
- practise rolling a ball
- practise intercepting a ball.

Resources and class management

Children work in groups of three. Each group will need one medium-sized rubber ball.

What to do

Explain to the children that in each group of three, two of them will roll a ball to each other and the third member of the group will run from a distance and try to intercept the ball halfway.

Each group of children should position themselves in a triangle with approximately seven or eight strides between each player. It is helpful when explaining the game to the children if you number each player 1, 2 and 3. Player 1 will be holding the ball with one hand (or both if necessary) on their preferred side, with the same leg back and their weight on the back foot. Tell them to swing the ball back, then bring their arm forwards and, at the same time, bend their trunk forward and transfer the weight to the front foot as the ball is released along the ground towards player 2. As

the ball is released, the third player in each group should run as fast as they can towards the path of the ball and, if they reach it in time, scoop it up using both hands, before rolling it back to player 1 again. Advise player 3 that if they are running very quickly and manage to scoop up the ball, it is best if they keep running for a few more steps in order to slow down gradually rather than trying to stop suddenly. When scooping the ball up, the children should reach forward with their hands and bend down from the waist, with their knees bending slightly. Let each player stay in the same position for several attempts before changing over, so that every child experiences each part of the activity. If the ball reaches player 2, tell the children to repeat the activity as before.

Differentiation

With younger or less able children, reduce the distance between each player to maybe only four or five strides and use larger balls, which will roll at a slower speed and will be easier to control.

Older or more able children can use a smaller ball and increase the distance between the players.

Now or later

Overarm throwing could be substituted for the rolling action. Make sure the children remember to put the same arm and leg back before pushing the ball from the shoulder rather than swinging the arm over as in a cricket bowling action. The third player should try and run in and catch the ball – tell them to watch it carefully from the time it leaves the hands of player 1.

Triangles

Objectives

To enable children to:
- practise underarm and overarm throwing
- practise stumping a wicket
- work co-operatively in a group.

Cross-curricular links

PSHE
Taking and sharing responsibility.

Dance
Changing level and direction of movement.

Resources and class management

Children work in groups of three. Each group will need a medium-sized rubber ball and a skittle or similar target which will stand upright.

What to do

Each group of three should collect one ball and one skittle between them. They should place the skittle upright on the ground Ask the children to number themselves 1, 2, and 3 within the group and to form a triangle, with player 2 standing in front of the skittle. Player 1 should have the ball and be facing player 2 about five paces away; player 3 should complete the triangle approximately five paces away from the others.

Explain to the children that player 1 will throw an underarm throw to player 2, who will touch the skittle with the ball before throwing overarm to player 3, who returns the ball overarm to player 1. At this point, remind the children that whichever throw they are doing they should have the same leg and foot back as the throwing arm they are using. Player 1 should release the ball at or just below shoulder height so that player 2 can stretch out their arms and catch the ball at just below chest height before turning and touching the skittle with the ball. Player 2 will need to be reminded that their feet and arms will need to be adjusted before throwing overarm from their preferred shoulder to player 3. Player 3 catches the ball before adjusting their feet and arms to return the ball overarm to player 1. If at any point during the activity the ball is dropped, tell the children that the intended receiver should run to pick up the ball before returning to their place and continuing the activity. Encourage the children to swap roles after a few turns, so that they each try all the parts of the activity.

Differentiation

With younger children this activity can be practised with just two children: player 1 throws to player 2, who turns and touches the skittle with the ball, then throws overarm back to player 1.

Now or later

When the children are familiar with this activity, tell player 2 to stand with their back to the skittle and, instead of striking the skittle with the ball, encourage them to see if they can move the ball around to the back of their body and touch the skittle without looking at it, before throwing the ball on. (See 'Roll and hold', Section 1, page 9)

Beanbag and hoop catch

Resources and class management

Children work in groups of four. Each group will need four beanbags and one small hoop, or alternatively small balls and containers can be used. You will also need skittles for the 'Now or later' activity.

What to do

Ask the children to find a partner, then tell them to go and join another pair to form a four. Each child should collect a beanbag, and one child in the group should collect a small hoop. They should put the hoop on the ground and form a circle around it – at this point you will see how far the children are from the hoop. If they are too near tell them to take approximately 3–4 strides backwards, but still retaining a circle.

Explain that they are going to take it in turns to throw the beanbag underarm to try and get it inside the hoop. As they throw, they can score one point every time they succeed in throwing the beanbag inside the hoop. Remind the children that right-handers should stand with their right foot back and left-handers should stand with their left foot back, and that they should not retrieve their beanbag until all four of them have thrown.

Objectives

To enable children to:

- practise aiming at a target
- improve their stance for underarm throwing
- co-operate in a small group.

Cross-curricular links

Gymnastics
Linking actions.

Dance
Controlling movements by varying tension.

Differentiation
The distance from the hoop can be made progressively larger so that more able children have to throw longer distances. Equally, the circle can be made smaller if children find it too hard.

Now or later
The hoop could be replaced with a smaller target such as a skittle when the children are more confident with this activity. Children should make sure that their right foot is back if they are right-handed and their left foot is back if they are left-handed. The throwing arm should be pulled back as far as possible. A suitable follow-up activity is 'Hoop Bounce' (page 31).

Bat-hand ball

Objectives
To enable children to:
- practise striking a ball
- practise underarm bowling
- practise retrieving a ball.

Cross-curricular links
PSHE
Agreeing and following rules for a group.

Resources and class management
Children work in groups of three. Each group will need a small, soft ball (preferably sponge or plastic). You will need small wooden bats for the 'Differentiation' activity, and a stopwatch with a second hand and copies of photocopiable page 57 ('Name the equipment') for the 'Now or later' activities.

What to do
Ask the children to form groups of three and to collect one ball between each group. Stand each group in a triangle, with player 1 holding the ball and facing player 2 and player 3 at the third point of the triangle. Each player should be approximately four paces away from the others. Explain to the children that player 1 will be the bowler (throwing underarm), player 2 the batsman, using their preferred hand to hit the ball, and player 3 will field, or retrieve the ball when it has been hit.

Remind the children that, when they are bowling or batting the ball, right-handers should have their right arm and right leg back, with their weight on the back foot; left-handers should have their left arm and leg back. The bowlers should aim for the appropriate side of the child who is batting. The batters should be standing sideways on to the bowler, with their preferred hand (the hand that would be used to hold a bat) raised to shoulder height and elbow bent with palm of the hand flat facing the ball, ready to use the hand as a bat and hit the ball as it approaches. Player 3 should be standing ready, so that if the ball is hit by player 2 they can run quickly, bend down when they are close to the ball on the ground and scoop it up. Make sure they are aware that it is OK to try and run and catch the ball before it reaches the ground. Once they have retrieved the ball, they should adjust their position and return the ball over- or underarm to player 1 who repeats the bowling action a further two or three times. Give each player a number of chances to hit the ball before changing over to play in a different position.

Differentiation
Younger children can begin this activity in pairs, and just practise the bowling and batting. Older or more able children can progress to using a circular wooden bat to hit the ball.

Now or later

- When the children can hit the ball every time with their hand you could set them the task of hitting accurately in the direction of player 3 who is fielding the ball. Tell them that they should aim to hit high enough and far enough so that player 3 can run and catch the ball easily. This is a good activity to encourage the children to place the ball accurately, as they will need this skill in rounders at a later stage.
- Back in the classroom, use photocopiable page 57 ('Name the equipment') to reinforce learning from the main part of the lesson.

In and out of the hoop

Objectives
To enable children to:
- improve speed when catching a beanbag
- practise a variety of throws
- work co-operatively with others.

Resources and class management

Children work in groups of four. Each group will need two large hoops and one beanbag between them.

What to do

Ask the children in their groups of four to place the two hoops four strides apart and number themselves 1 to 4. Explain that this practice requires speed and quick reactions. Player 1 and player 2 should stand one in each hoop, with player 1 holding a beanbag; players 3 and 4 should stand four strides to the side of players 1 and 2 respectively.

Tell the children that player 1 will throw the beanbag underarm to player 2, who should catch it and throw it upwards high in the air before stepping quickly outside the hoop. Whilst the beanbag is in the air, player 4 runs into the hoop and catches it, before throwing it underarm to player 1. Player 1 catches the beanbag, then throws it upwards high in the air as before, stepping out of the hoop to enable player 3 to run in and catch the beanbag. Player 3 throws underarm to player 4 who repeats the sequence as before. This can continue until the children can judge how high to throw the beanbag and when to commence their run.

Differentiation

Younger or less able children can do this practice without the underarm throwing: each group of children will need two beanbags instead of one. Player 1 throws the beanbag high in the air then steps outside the hoop to enable player 3 to run in and catch it. At the same time player 2 throws up their beanbag and steps outside the hoop to enable player 4 to run in and catch it before repeating. Effectively this activity is done in pairs until the children are confident enough to work in a four.

Encourage older children to build up speed in this practice so that immediately after they catch the beanbag they throw it into the air.

Now or later

When the children are catching the beanbag from the underarm throw each time, introduce a competitive element by giving them a two-minute timed session to see how many times the beanbag can travel around all four players. Each group counts 1 when the beanbag has travelled in the sequence 1 to 2 to 4 to 3 to 2.

Net and wall games
Skills for one or two players

The games that follow in this section cover practice for all short tennis activities and wall games. They should normally be used in the summer term and can be carried out on the playing field, the playground or other hard-surfaced area, or in the school hall. If you have no access to a large expanse of plain wall, the activities can sometimes be adapted. If this is the case it will be stated in the individual activity (see 'Resources and class management'). Distances between children in the activities are suggestions only and can be readily adjusted according to the age and ability of the class.

The photocopiable pages can be used as an extension of the activities in this section, or can be used as stand-alone worksheets back in the classroom to support vocabulary and learning from PE lessons.

Photocopiable page 59 ('What can I do?' chart) can be used when children are familiar with the activities to reinforce language and to let them plot their progress through the activities over the course of the term or year.

The activities in this section focus on:

- hitting a ball accurately
- practising underarm throwing
- practising aiming at a point in space or a target
- keeping a ball in motion
- working co-operatively
- returning a ball to another player.

Handball

Objectives

To enable children to:

- practise keeping a ball moving
- practise batting skills
- work co-operatively.

Cross-curricular links

PSHE

Taking and sharing responsibility.

Resources and class management

Children work in pairs. Each pair will need one small soft ball made of plastic, sponge, or very lightweight rubber between them. This activity is best practised on a hard playground surface or a hall floor.

What to do

Ask the children to collect one ball between each pair and to stand facing one another five or six strides apart. Explain that they are going to bat the ball between each other using their hand, and that they must try to keep the ball moving back and forth for as long as possible. Tell the child with the ball to drop it in front of them, and as it bounces back up to swing their preferred arm back and hit the ball with a flat palm; they should try to lift the ball slightly as they do so to give their partner extra time to return the ball. Those who are receiving the ball should watch it carefully before moving to a position which is just behind the ball in the air, and trying to hit it back with the flat palm of their preferred hand, again lifting the ball slightly to enable a good return from their partner. Emphasize the importance of lifting the ball to enable it to be passed between the two players a number of times. Remind the children that if they are hitting with the right hand, their right leg and arm should be back, and if hitting with the left hand, the left leg and arm should be back.

Differentiation

If this activity takes place in a school hall using plastic balls, it is easier for younger children if they let the ball bounce once after it has been hit to give them a longer time to position themselves to hit it. Younger children who find this practice difficult outside can try standing beside their partner and alternately hitting the ball upwards,

trying to keep it in the air.

Older or more able children can be given a target number to try and reach – say four repetitions to begin with, gradually building up to the target number. Older or more able children should also be encouraged to turn their body sideways as they hit the ball; they may need reminding to move the feet as they turn the body sideways.

Now or later

This activity can progress to children using a bat to hit the ball; if so, they should stand double the distance apart and use a lightweight rubber ball that will bounce in between each hit.

Double bounce

Objectives

To enable children to:

- practise sustained concentration
- practise watching a ball carefully
- practise hitting a ball

Cross-curricular links

PSHE

Recognizing how behaviour affects other people.

Resources and class management

Children work independently. Each child will need a bat and a small ball – the bats can be of any size, but should preferably have a flat surface, and the ball can be of any material. This activity is best practised on a playground or other smooth surface.

What to do

Ask the children to find themselves a space and to hold their bat in one hand and the ball in the other. Explain that when they start they are going to throw the ball straight up in the air and let it bounce once on the ground before using their bat to hit the ball high in the air again, letting it bounce once more and repeating. Tell the children that they should try and keep the ball moving for as long as possible without losing control of it. They should wait until the ball has reached the highest part of its bounce before placing the bat, flat side upwards, underneath the ball; as the ball touches the bat they should lift it in a straight line upwards before letting it bounce again. Explain that they may move their feet if necessary in order to keep the ball going straight up in the air, but they should aim to keep their feet as still as possible. When the children have practised this for a suitable length of time, encourage them to count how many times they can complete the action without losing control of the ball and to try and beat their own score each time.

Differentiation

Younger children will find this activity easier if they begin by using their hand instead of a bat.

Now or later

When the children are familiar with this activity they can practise it in pairs. They should stand side by side, sharing a ball, but with a bat each. Player 1 throws the ball up into the air and lets it bounce, then player 2 repeats, and lets it bounce again before player 1 continues. Explain that it is important that they lift the ball high enough and straight enough to give their partner a better chance of lifting it easily. This activity encourages the children to work together.

Flat hand walk

Objectives

To enable children to:
- increase skills using a ball and bat
- sustain concentration levels
- improve body awareness.

Cross-curricular links

Gymnastics

Choosing and linking skills and actions.

PSHE

Agreeing and following rules for a group or class.

Resources and class management

Children work independently. Each child will need a small ball made of sponge, plastic, or lightweight rubber. This activity will need a large open space, and you will need two lines marked at opposite ends of the area, ideally 10–15 metres apart.

What to do

Ask the children to form one long line standing side by side, all facing the same direction. Tell them to place their ball on the palm of their hand (it doesn't matter which), and keep the hand flat and open. Explain that they should extend the arm holding the ball until it is straight out in front of their body. Keeping the arm straight and the hand flat and open, tell them to walk straight ahead until they reach the line on the other side of the area. They must resist the temptation to close their fingers around the ball, or to bend the arm at the elbow. When the children reach the line they can return to their original position holding the ball in one hand, before trying the activity again. Finally, after trying this two or three times, encourage them to begin walking at a faster pace, and eventually running, but always encourage a flat hand and a straight arm.

Differentiation

To help younger children resist the temptation to close their hand around the ball, use a medium-sized rubber ball which cannot be held in this way. Older children can also use a larger ball if necessary.

Now or later

When the children can do this activity with some skill, you can make it into a competitive team activity. Make teams of four children with one ball between them. Tell them to line up in their teams one behind another, with the front player holding the ball and all the children facing the same direction. On your command, the players with the ball walk or run as fast as they can towards the line without losing the ball. They should then close their hand around the ball, run back to the next player, hand them the ball and join the end of the team. All the time emphasize the importance of balancing the ball on a flat palm rather than holding the ball whilst running.

Bouncy walk

Resources and class management

Children work independently. Each child will need a small bat with a flat surface and a small ball of any kind. This activity is best practised on a playground or other smooth surface. You will also need copies of photocopiable page 60 ('What does it do?') for the 'Now or later' activity.

What to do

Explain to the children that in this activity they are going to walk forwards slowly, at the same time hitting their ball down towards the ground and repeating this every time the ball bounces up. The important points to emphasize in doing this are connected with the way the ball is hit. Encourage the children to try and hit the ball in a straight line down towards the ground so that it bounces up in a straight line – if they keep their body weight over their front foot it will help them to do this. Right-handers should lead with their left foot, and left-handers with their right foot before they begin walking. The children will have more control in this activity if they watch the way the ball bounces upwards after it has hit the ground and try to hit it when it is at the highest point of the bounce. Very young children may find this difficult at the start but will soon begin to watch the ball with some purpose. They should be encouraged not to forget to look where they are going!

Differentiation

Younger children can try this activity on the spot at first, and can progress to walking when they have some skill in bouncing the ball successfully.

Older children can be encouraged to run while bouncing the ball; if they begin to lose control over the bouncing action, return to slow walking until they have improved.

Now or later

This is a suitable activity to encourage children to use their non-preferred hand for a short time. Explain to them that at a later stage, when they play team games, it is an asset to be able to use the non-preferred hand to throw, hit or catch a ball.

After the lesson, introduce the children to photocopiable page 60 ('What does it do?') which will reinforce the vocabulary connected with using the new equipment they have been introduced to during PE lessons.

Objectives

To enable children to:

- develop accuracy in ball skills
- use a bat effectively
- move fluently whilst controlling a ball.

Cross-curricular links

Gymnastics

Developing the range of skills and actions including balancing.

Throw, bounce and catch

Resources and class management

Children work individually. Each child will need a small ball that will bounce easily. You will need access to a high wall and a piece of chalk for this activity.

What to do

Ask the children each to collect a ball and to stand in a row, approximately ten strides away from the wall. Explain that they are going to throw the ball underarm towards the wall, aiming higher than head height, allowing the ball to bounce once before catching it. If they throw the ball high it will slow down the return of the ball and enable them to catch it more easily. Remind them that right-handers must place their right arm and leg back, with the weight on the back foot initially; left-handers

Objectives

To enable children to:

- practise aiming skills
- practise underarm throwing skills
- retrieve a ball from a bounce.

Cross-curricular links

PSHE

Agreeing and following rules for a group or class.

should place the left arm and leg back. As the ball is thrown the weight should be transferred to the front foot. Encourage the children to try and catch the ball after it has bounced only once – remind them to watch the ball carefully and extend their arms with hands together and fingers spread, then to pull the ball into the body as they catch it. Finally, tell the children that they will almost certainly have to run to catch the ball after it has bounced.

Differentiation

Tell younger children to throw the ball much higher than their own head in order to slow down its progress. If they find this difficult they can let the ball bounce several times on the ground before it is retrieved.

Older children can throw directly at the wall at head level.

Now or later

When the children have improved their skills, use a piece of chalk to draw circles on the wall so that they have to aim for the circle when they throw the ball. To encourage them, tell them to count one point every time they are successful in hitting the target.

Bat and ball shuttle

Objectives

To enable children to:
- improve ball skills
- speed up footwork
- work co-operatively with a partner.

Cross-curricular links

PSHE
Setting simple goals.

Gymnastics
Linking skills and actions in short movement phrases.

Resources and class management

Children work in pairs. Each child will need a plastic bat with a rim on the outside or a tennis racket, and one small ball between them.

What to do

Ask the children to form pairs, collect one bat each and a ball between them, and to stand facing each other approximately ten strides apart. If you wish, line the class up in two rows ten strides apart, so that each child is facing their partner. Explain to the children that the player with the ball should put it on the flat side of their bat and hold it at arm's length, then walk or run slowly towards their partner, trying to keep the ball as still as possible on their bat. When they arrive at their partner they should tip the bat gently and let the ball roll onto their partner's bat, also being held at arm's length and with the flat side uppermost. When the ball is successfully on the bat player 2 walks quickly, balancing the ball on the bat, and stops when they reach the position that player 1 occupied. If the ball rolls off the bat, either when the player is moving or when it is being transferred to the other bat, then the children should be instructed to pick it up and put it back on the bat. Finally, player 2 walks or runs towards player 1 and repeats the action as before.

Differentiation

Younger or less able children can do this activity using only one bat. When player 1 reaches player 2 after balancing the ball on the bat, the ball can be taken off the bat by player 2 who then holds the ball and runs back with it to replace player 1.

Now or later

When children can do this activity without dropping the ball too many times, encourage a competitive element by letting the pairs join with another pair and make a race of the activity.

NET AND WALL GAMES
GROUP ACTIVITIES FOR THREE PLAYERS OR MORE

The activities in this section focus on:
- hitting a ball accurately
- practising underarm throwing
- practising aiming at a point in space or a target
- keeping a ball in motion
- working co-operatively
- returning a ball to another player.

CROSS THE CIRCLE

OBJECTIVES
To enable children to:
- practise racket skills
- improve ball control
- increase accuracy.

CROSS-CURRICULAR LINKS
PSHE

Recognizing how behaviour affects other people.

GYMNASTICS

Finding space and using it safely.

RESOURCES AND CLASS MANAGEMENT
Children work in groups of four. Each group will need one small lightweight ball made of plastic or sponge. You will need copies of photocopiable page 55 ('My progress chart') for the 'Now or later' activity.

WHAT TO DO
Ask the children to form groups of four, collect one ball between each group and find a space. They should hold hands to form a circle, then release hands and take one step back (you can make adjustments to the circle size if necessary). Tell the child with the ball that they should throw underarm to the player opposite them in the circle. The child receiving the ball must use a flat hand as a bat to try and hit the ball back to the thrower. When player 1 receives the ball back they should pass it on to the player on their right, who will throw underarm across the circle to the player opposite them, who will again use their hand as a bat and return the ball from where it came; the player receiving the ball passes to the player on the right and so on. The children should repeat this sequence for as long as possible; tell them that if the ball goes out of play the child who threw the ball is responsible for retrieving it. Encourage the children who are hitting to stand sideways on to strike the ball and to lift it slightly to gain some height – this will help improve accuracy when returning the ball.

DIFFERENTIATION
All children will benefit from beginning this activity as a 'throw and catch' practice, without the 'batting' element. This has the advantage that the children will become familiar with the rules and keep the ball in play for longer.

Now or later

When the children have developed some skill at hitting the ball, encourage them to count one point each time they successfully hit it and to keep a personal record (see photocopiable page 55, 'My progress chart'). When you repeat this activity, remind the children to check their records and try and improve on it.

Batting threes

Objectives

To enable children to:
- improve racket skills
- practise underarm throwing
- practise accurately placing a ball.

Cross-curricular links

Dance

Changing the direction of movements.

Resources and class management

Children work in groups of three. Each group will need one small plastic tennis racket and one lightweight ball. It is helpful to practise this activity with a net or other waist-high obstacle which a number of children can use at the same time, but the activity is useful without access to a net.

What to do

Ask the children to collect one racket and one ball between each group of three and to number themselves 1, 2 and 3. Player 1 holds the racket and stands on the opposite side of the net to players 2 and 3; player 2 holds the ball and stands facing player 1. Player 3 should be available to retrieve any loose ball, and should stand on the same side of the net as player 2.

Explain to the children that player 2 should throw the ball underarm over the net, and player 1 will let it bounce once before trying to hit it back over the net. Player 3 retrieves the ball before throwing underarm to player 2, who repeats the action. Remind the children that throwers and hitters should have their right hand and right foot back, or left hand and left foot back as appropriate. Players with the racket should stand sideways on as they hit the ball; encourage them to swing the racket back and, on hitting the ball, allow the racket to follow the ball for some distance whilst still retaining a hold on it. Point out to the children who are throwing that they should throw in such a way that they make it as easy as possible for those with the rackets to hit the ball. After several attempts, rotate the children so that they all have a chance at all the parts of the task.

Differentiation

Younger children can use their hand as a racket in the initial stages and dispense with the net.

Now or later

When children are more confident, encourage those with a racket to try and place the ball by hitting it towards the retriever or the player who is throwing underarm. More able children will find that they must move their feet quickly in order to be in a position to hit towards a spot.

Ball in the air

Objectives

To enable children to:
- increase concentration span
- improve ball control
- practise batting skills.

Resources and class management

Children work in groups of four. Each group will need one small lightweight ball made of plastic or sponge.

What to do

Ask each group of four children to collect one ball between them and stand in a circle with some space on either side of each player. Explain to the children that each group will begin this activity in a circle, but as they progress, it is likely that they will lose the circle formation. Ask the child with the ball to throw it upwards into the air, then to step backwards to enable the child to their left to hit the ball upwards with the palm of the hand as it falls to approximately waist height. Once the ball falls again to waist height, the child to the left of the player who hit the ball runs to hit it upwards. This continues, with each player in the group taking a turn to hit the ball upwards with the palm of the hand, then stepping away to allow the next child in to hit the ball. Emphasize the fact that children will have to watch the ball very carefully and run quickly in order to hit the ball. Point out that as they run forward they should try and control their movements so that the ball is hit upwards as accurately as possible. If the ball is dropped, the player who hit it is responsible for retrieving it.

Differentiation

Younger or less able children can begin this activity by working in pairs side by side, then increasing the number to three and finally four players.

Older children can be encouraged to count the number of times they can successfully hit the ball before it falls to the ground.

Now or later

Very able children can try this activity using plastic rackets, but warn them that the effort needed to hit the ball upwards is reduced when using a racket. Emphasize ball and bat control at all times.

Cross-curricular links

PSHE

Recognizing how their behaviour affects other people.

High and low

Resources and class management

Children work in groups of four. Each group will need one small ball such as a tennis ball or rubber ball. You will also need a long net (such as a tennis net or similar), or two gymnastics benches on top of one another with the widest surfaces together.

What to do

Ask the children to collect one ball between each group of four. Tell them to arrange themselves with two players on each side of the net; they should be standing approximately three or four strides apart on each side of the net. Explain to the player with the ball that they should throw underarm to one of the players on the opposite side of the net, and it is their choice whether they throw the

Objectives

To enable children to:

- work co-operatively
- practise accuracy when throwing a ball
- learn techniques associated with nets.

Cross-curricular links

PSHE

Playing and working co-operatively.

ball so that it just clears the net or whether they throw so that the ball goes very high over the net. When the player receiving the ball has caught it or retrieved it they throw underarm to one of the players on the opposite side of the net, again making a choice about the height of the throw. Remind all the players that right-handers should throw with the right foot back and left-handers with the left foot back. Tell the children that if they wish to throw low over the net they should release the ball early during their swing – at approximately waist height; and if they wish to throw high over the net, the ball should be released later. Remind the children that this is an activity for four children and that they should try and involve all the players in their group. Equally, this is a practice involving high and low throwing over a net, so encourage the children to use both heights regularly as they throw. Finally, tell the children to try and keep the ball in play for as long as possible, but if the ball is not caught it should be retrieved by the player receiving it.

Differentiation

Give less able or younger children a sequence of throws, so that they know whether the next throw is high or low and which player it should go to. Older children who are catching the ball easily should be encouraged to speed up the activity by throwing the ball as soon as they receive it from a player.

Now or later

This activity can also be done with a bounce throw instead of an underarm throw. The players throwing the ball should aim to bounce it on the opposite side of the net from which they are standing, and the player receiving the ball must wait until it has bounced before reaching out with cupped hands to catch it.

Up in the sky

Objectives

To enable children to:
- practise throwing a ball accurately in the air
- work co-operatively
- practise receiving a ball.

Cross-curricular links

Gymnastics
Linking skills and actions in short movement phrases.

PSHE
Taking and sharing responsibility.

Resources and class management

Children work in groups of three. Each group will need one small ball composed of any material. You will need small plastic rackets for the 'Now or later' activity.

What to do

Ask the children to collect one ball between each group of three. Tell them to stand in a line, side by side, with approximately one stride between each player; the ball should be held by one of the players at either end of the line of three. Explain to the children that the ball is going to be thrown upwards, but towards the next player in line so that it can be easily caught by that player. When the ball has been caught they

should throw it up in the air again and towards the third player, who will catch it and repeat the same action back along the row again. Emphasize that the main focus of the activity is to place the ball in the air accurately so that it drops near enough to the receiving player so that it can be caught without them needing to move their feet. Remind the children that when catching the ball they should stretch their arms upwards and cup their hands together with fingers spread, and as the ball is caught they should pull it towards the centre of the body. Let the children practise this activity for long enough to link the throwing and catching together to make a smooth sequence of movements.

Differentiation

Younger children can practise this activity standing side by side with no gap between the players – this simplifies the throwing movement to one of an upwards-only throw.

Now or later

When the children have some degree of control and accuracy, this activity can be practised in pairs with one player holding a small plastic racket. Tell the children to stand side by side with one player holding the ball and the other the racket. The player with the ball throws it upwards, and the player with the racket tries to hit it downwards towards the ground. The player who hits the ball then retrieves it and returns to their position. Repeat this activity with the players changing equipment after every two or three turns.

Throwing circle

Objectives

To enable children to:
- increase accuracy in ball skills
- practise underarm throwing
- practise catching at speed.

Cross-curricular links

PSHE

Identifying and respecting the similarities and differences between people.

Dance

Changing speed, level and direction of movement.

Resources and class management

Children work in groups of four. Each group will need one tennis ball or other small ball. You will need photocopiable page 61 ('What am I doing?') for 'Now or later'.

What to do

Ask the children form a group of four, and to collect a tennis ball between each group. Tell them to hold hands in a circle, then release their hands and take two steps backwards. Explain that they are going to throw the ball underarm around the circle as quickly and as accurately as they can. Emphasize that if the ball is not caught they must slow their throwing down until the ball is being caught each time again. Before they begin, tell them that they will be catching the ball from the right and throwing to the left, and that this will necessitate moving their feet before throwing. Also remind the children that right-handers should throw with their right arm and foot back, and left-handers with their left arm and foot back. Finally, tell the children that you are looking for smooth accurate actions when they are throwing and catching.

Differentiation

In preparation for this activity younger children can begin in groups of three, then progress to groups of four. Older or more able children should be encouraged to do this activity in both directions – throwing to the left around the circle, then changing to throwing to the right around the circle every so often.

Now or later

Tell the children to throw with their non-preferred hand, but to continue catching with both hands cupped. Throwing in this way is a useful skill when they begin to serve in tennis at a later stage. Photocopiable page 61 ('What am I doing?') can be used back in the classroom to reinforce learning.

Section 5 MINI-GAMES AND CREATIVE GAMES

The activities in this section focus on
- working co-operatively in small groups
- using a variety of equipment
- encouraging leadership skills
- using simple rules within a game
- practising hitting a target
- encouraging competition.

The National Curriculum states that children at Key Stage 1 should 'play simple, competitive net, striking/fielding and invasion-type games that they and others have made, using simple tactics for attacking and defending'. These games need not be modified versions of full team games, which is required at Key Stage 2, but should be activities which encourage children to work together and sometimes against each other using the skills that they have been learning in the lessons. Many of the activities in Sections 2, 3 and 4 can easily be adapted to make them competitive, and some ideas for these adaptations can be found in the 'Now or later' sections of the lesson plans.

WHEN TO USE MINI-GAMES

Children in the early years of their physical development may progress in very different ways – some children gaining co-ordination skills quickly, others still having difficulty with activities which require these skills at the end of the first year. Simple running games will probably have been played from the start, but before mini-games are introduced it is essential that the children have some experience of the basic activities of throwing, catching and using space. If you are teaching these skills with progression on a regular basis then it is only one step further to adapt the group activities in Sections 2, 3 and 4 and make the activities into mini-games after the children have gained some skills in a practice situation.

WHEN TO USE CREATIVE GAMES

Creative games – games which the children themselves have helped to make up – are a useful tool for encouraging co-operative work, and for helping children to come to an understanding of rules, their purpose and application. Creative games can be introduced as something that you do once a half-term or term during the course of one lesson, or you can set aside a block of lessons and let the children create and experience several of their own or others' games.

Organization of mini-games and creative games

When mini-games or creative games are to be played, a lesson should consist of a warm-up followed by skill activities, the mini-game or activity itself, and a cooling-down session. If the lesson time is very short or the children are slow to respond to instructions, the skill activities part of the lesson can be shortened in order to accommodate the teaching of the mini-games.

Playing a mini-game

Objectives

To enable children to:

- work in small groups
- use a variety of equipment
- follow simple rules.

Cross-curricular links

PSHE

Working co-operatively and teamwork.

Resources and class management

Children work in groups of up to four. You will need equipment appropriate to the mini-game you are playing.

What to do

When you wish to include mini-games in a lesson, consideration should be given to the number of children in each group, the equipment available, and the rules of the mini-game. Children at this level of skill need to have as much hands-on experience as is possible, so groups should be kept small and numbers should not rise above four versus four for any one activity. This enables children in each group to take an active part in the game from the start.

The equipment for playing a mini-game should be kept simple. Goalposts can be created using upright equipment such as skittles, and other equipment could include skipping ropes placed on the ground in circles or lines, buckets in which to throw balls or quoits, chalk marks on the ground or on a wall drawn by the teacher to show goal areas, as well as various-sized hoops which can be placed flat on the ground in order that children can bounce or throw balls into the centre of them.

Rules of the mini-game need to be clearly emphasized before it commences. It often helps if you ask a small group of children to show the rest of the class how they are going to play the game. Let the group step through the activity as they would play it, and as they do so you should focus on the rules that they need to play the game.

Differentiation

Children could be placed in mixed-ability groups to allow less able children to be supported by those who have a better understanding of the rules of the game.

Now or later

Play the mini-games on a number of occasions, using similar teams if possible, and see if the children can beat or improve their scores as they gain more practice at the skills. You could organize a league championship over the course of a term to encourage children.

Making a creative game

Objectives
To enable children to:
- work in a small group to create a game
- use simple rules effectively.

Cross-curricular links
PSHE
Working co-operatively in teams.

English
Instructional writing.

Resources and class management
Children should work in the classroom in groups of four. You will need large blank sheets of paper, or enlarged copies of photocopiable page 62 ('Creating a game').

What to do
Although children will be actively involved in making up creative games, it would be too time consuming and counter-productive if they had to start from a blank canvas. Give groups some large pieces of blank, white paper, or enlarged copies of the 'Creating a game' worksheet (photocopiable page 62), and on each sheet put down some basic information for each group to begin.

The children should then work to create their game for teams of two or four children, using the photocopiable sheet as a structure for the rules of their game. If the children have not attempted this before, you may want to decide what equipment each group will be allowed to use, and write these on the photocopiable page before you give it to the children.

The sheet includes space for the name of the game, which the children themselves can make up; space to include some simple equipment that will be available for them to use, and details of the area in which they will play the game. From those details you should give each group a short time to decide how the equipment is to be used, how goals are going to be scored and what the rules are going to be. It is a good idea to suggest at the outset that the children decide on the skills (such as throwing, bouncing or kicking) that their game will concentrate on, and no more than three rules. You can decide whether to put the children into groups yourself or let the children decide for themselves.

Differentiation
Children can work in mixed-ability groups to allow support for less able writers, who can still make contributions to ideas for the rules of the game. You may wish to provide suggestions for rules or equipment as a starting point for some groups, or ask older or more able children to concentrate on working specific skills into their game.

Now or later
Groups can share their ideas for games with others in the class, and refine their suggestions if they wish. When the children are happy with their rules, save them for another lesson and start to play the games as a class.

Playing a creative game

Objectives

To enable children to:
- use a variety of equipment
- play games competitively
- interpret simple rules within a game
- use leadership and teamwork skills.

Cross-curricular links

PSHE

Working in a team and co-operating.

Resources and class management

Children work in teams of two or four, playing in a large, open area such as the playground. You will need the children's completed copies of photocopiable page 62, equipment appropriate to the creative games you are playing, coloured armbands.

What to do

When the children have created their games and are ready to begin playing them, begin with some warm-up activities (see Section 1). When they are thoroughly warmed-up, tell them to get into their groups for the game (these groups may have been decided when the games were planned, or you could choose groups as appropriate) and direct each group to an area of the playground. Ask each child in the group to number themselves 1, 2, 3 and 4. Numbers 1 and 2 should collect the equipment necessary for playing the game (the bats, balls, or beanbags); number 3 should collect the equipment needed to score a goal and put it in position according to the pitch layout (this could be a bucket, two cones for goalposts, or skittles set up in formation); and number 4 should collect two sets of coloured armbands which will be worn by the individual team members to distinguish who is playing against who. Before you send the children to their areas to start playing the game, ask groups to nominate one member to act as 'referee' whilst still taking part in the game.

When you have started all the groups off playing their games, move between the groups to make sure that everything is working smoothly. You may want to choose one specific aspect of playing the games (such as throwing, bouncing or kicking the ball correctly, using as much of the space as possible, or keeping to the rules of the game) and concentrate on this skill with each group in turn. If you find that all the groups are having similar problems, stop the class and clarify the problem with the whole class before allowing the groups to carry on with their games.

When the children have finished playing their games, make sure that you ask the children what scores were achieved within each group (these could be recorded and the children could try to beat their scores on another occasion). The cooling-down activity should be done at the end of the lesson as normal.

Differentiation

Children should work in the same mixed-ability groups as they did when they were planning their games.

Now or later

See if the children can beat their scores for the game on another occasion. After the children have tried actually playing their games, do they want to make any changes to the rules of their game to make it better?

Name Date

My warm-up chart	
Activity	**Teacher's signature**
Roll and hold	
Roll and run	
Underarm duo	
Throw and catch	
Bouncing Bonanza	
Hoop la!	
Figure of 8 sprint	
Whistle stop	
Rolling rings	
Quoit throw	

Ask your teacher to sign when they think you can do each activity really well.

Name Date

My progress chart							
Name of activity	**Duration** (time in minutes or seconds)	**My scores**					

Name Date

My body

Can you name the parts of the body? Use the words below.

leg	shoulder	hand	waist	arm	right foot	left foot

Use the words above and the words below to make sentences saying what you can do.

throw	kick	hit	bat	dribble

Name Date

Name the equipment

Use these words to name the pictures

tennis racket	small ball	football	bat
hockey stick	quoit	hoop	skipping rope

1. ______________ 2. ______________ 3. ______________

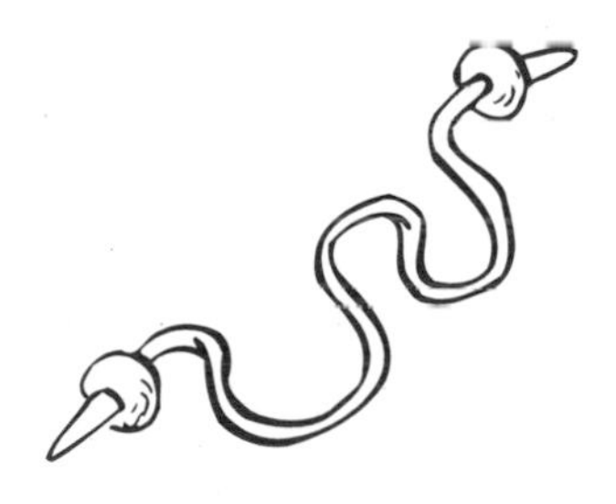

4. ______________ 5. ______________ 6. ______________

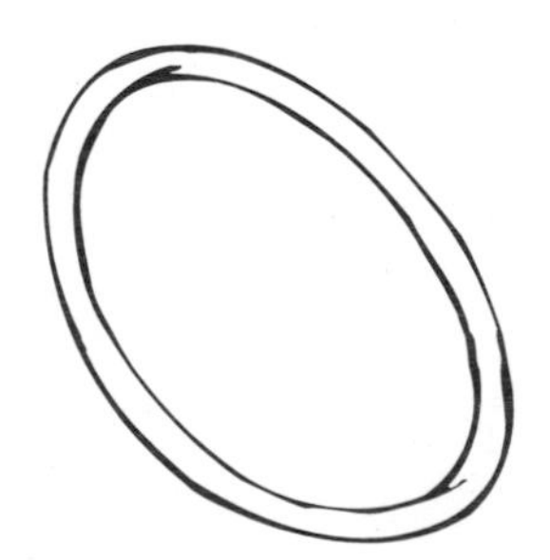

7. ______________ 8. ______________

Name Date

Find the mistakes

Put a circle around the things that you think are wrong in this picture.

Name Date

What can I do?

Draw what you have learned to do in the boxes below and write underneath what you call it.

I can ____________________

____

I can ____________________

____

I can ____________________

____

I can ____________________

____

I can ____________________

____

I can ____________________

____

Photocopiables

Name Date

What does it do?

Can you match the pictures of the equipment to the sentence saying what it is used for?

I can use it to hit a ball.

I can use it to bounce a ball.

I can dribble a ball with it.

I can kick it.

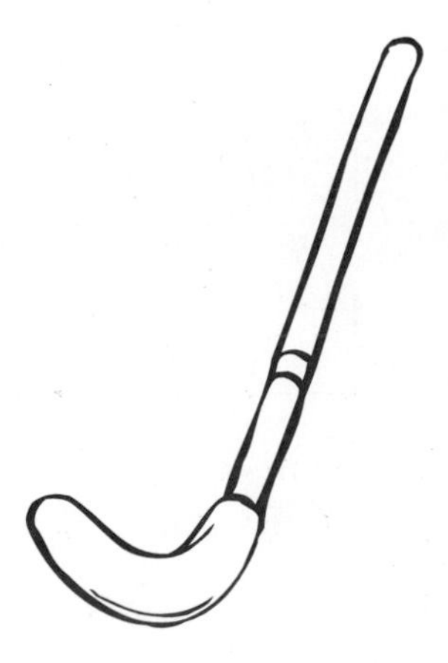

I can throw it.

Name Date

What am I doing?

Use the words below to finish the sentences that make the pictures correct.

throwing underarm	throwing overarm
kicking	hitting the ball	running

Name Date

Creating a game

Our game is called ____________________

There are [ ] people in each team.

Draw or write the pieces of equipment you will need

Draw the pitch here

Write down three rules for your game:

____

____

____

Goals are scored when ____________________

____

The winners are ____________________

Name Date

Certificate

This is to certify that

____

has successfully completed

____

____

Signed ___________________________________

Date _____________________________________

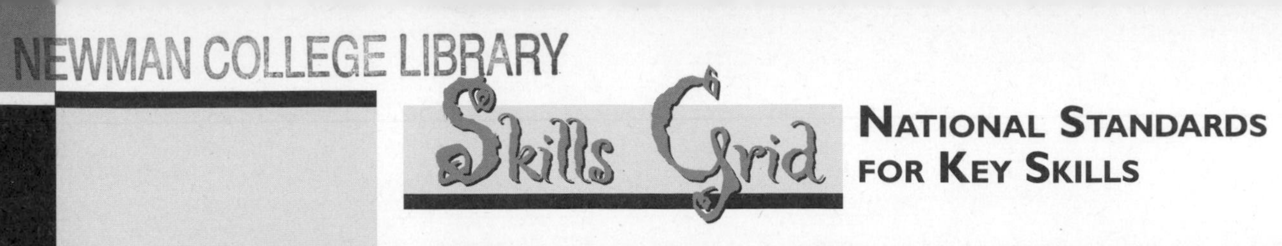

National Standards for Key Skills

Section	Skill	Underarm throwing	Overarm throwing	Rolling a ball	Catching	Kicking a ball	Hitting a ball	Retrieving a ball	Dodging and feinting	Using the space	Bouncing a ball	Aiming
Section 1 – Warm-up activities	Roll and hold			✔								
	Roll and run			✔				✔				
	Underarm duo	✔			✔							✔
	Throw and catch	✔			✔							
	Bouncing bonanza				✔						✔	
	Hoop la!									✔		
	Figure of 8 sprint									✔		
	Whistle stop									✔		
	Rolling rings	✔			✔							✔
	Quoit throw											✔
Section 2 – Invasion games	Kick, stop, kick					✔						
	Feint and dodge								✔			
	Long and short throwing		✔							✔		✔
	Figure of 8 dribble					✔				✔		
	Push the ball						✔			✔		
	Alternate bounce										✔	
	Count and throw	✔										
	Piggy in the middle roll			✔								
	Two versus two		✔						✔			
	Shuttle relay							✔		✔		
	Beanbag sprint											✔
	Shoot and hit		✔					✔				✔
Section 3 – Striking and fielding games	Wall bounce	✔						✔				✔
	Two throw quoits	✔			✔			✔				✔
	Hoop bounce				✔			✔				✔
	Run and retrieve			✔				✔				
	Bowl and bounce	✔			✔							
	Over and under	✔	✔									
	Skittle alley	✔						✔				✔
	Beat the ball			✔				✔				
	Triangles	✔	✔		✔							
	Beanbag and hoop catch	✔										✔
	Bat-hand ball	✔					✔	✔				
	In and out of the hoop	✔	✔		✔							
Section 4 – Net and wall games	Handball						✔					
	Double bounce						✔					
	Flat hand walk									✔		
	Bouncy walk									✔	✔	
	Throw, bounce and catch	✔			✔		✔	✔				✔
	Bat and ball shuttle										✔	
	Cross the circle	✔			✔							✔
	Batting threes	✔					✔					✔
	Ball in the air						✔					
	High and low	✔										✔
	Up in the sky	✔			✔			✔				
	Throwing circle	✔			✔							✔
Section 5 Mini-games	Playing a mini-game											
	Making a creative game											
	Playing a creative game											